VIEW FROM A HEARSE

LIGHTEN UP!

By Bruce Goddard

SpeakingDirect Publishing

Kennesaw, Georgia

© 2005, SpeakingDirect.com
3002 Windward Drive
Suite 200
Kennesaw, GA 30152

ISBN: 0-976770-0-2

DEDICATION

This book is dedicated to the memory of my parents, Ed and Naia Goddard. The memories of sitting together as a family in their bedroom reading the Bible would give me spiritual hunger and thirst. The sound of laughter in our home would cause me to want to see the lighter side of life.

In this book, you will get a little of both – funny and spiritual. There is no doubt that I got it from them.

I'm not sure if you give them credit for what you are about to read or you blame them. I am certain there are mixed opinions, and after you read this book, you will have yours.

I do know this. They were incredible human beings and wonderful parents. They both passed away before I gave my first speech. I've wished so many times that they could be in my audience.

Now, I'm wishing they could have read this book.

Somehow, I think they have done both.

ACKNOWLEDGEMENTS

There are a few people I need to thank for making the story within this book possible.

First and foremost, to my wife, Kathy, I thank you for allowing me to travel all over the place and do what's in my heart. You are always encouraging me to keep living on the edge out on a limb and outside of my comfort zone – to engage and touch hurting people. You are a true giver, a selfless human being, and I love you.

To David, John, and Luke, there is no way I can tell you how proud I am of each of you. All three of you have been great encouragers to me. It has been neat watching you grow up and walk through troubles of your own and come out on the other side stronger and better for it. This book is really for you. One day, when I'm dead and gone, I want you to be able to remember all the stories your dad told. Here they are. I don't think I've missed many of them. Let them become your stories. But more than that, in spite of my weaknesses and shortcomings, I want you to know my heart.

To Tami, I hope I don't embarrass you too much. You know I love you, and I will make you one heck of a daddy-in-law. You wait. You'll see.

To Kristy, Deanne and Adam, at different times each of you lived with us and became a part of our family. You saw who I really am – with all my warts and blemishes... and you loved me anyway. I learned from you, and I have written this for you as well.

To Mac, Kikky, and George, we have one thing in common that gives us the ability to handle most anything that comes our way. We had the best parents God ever created. God blessed us in an unbelievable way. Thank you for our wonderful lifelong relationship and love we share for each other. To Annis, Ken, and Jaye, you make them all better. Jaye, you will have a special crown for putting up with George.

To "Miss" Irene, you have never done anything but encourage me, and you are a great part of the emotion behind this book and a wonderful mother-in-law. To Jim and Lynn and Rusty and Mia, I feel like you all are my blood kin. Thanks for always laughing at my stories and encouraging me to write this book. To Rudy and Carol, what can I say? Thanks to Rudy for booking all the speaking engagements and making it profitable and pushing me to get this book done. Thanks to Carol for making sure some of the stories Rudy wanted to delete stayed in the book. A special thanks to Courtney and Claire – who helped with the editing and all the assistance with correspondence to our clients.

To the thousands of people who have been in my audience the last several years: From the stage, I watched you laugh and I watched you cry, and I was humbled as you stood on your feet many times and gave me loud applause. Because I saw that, I knew I had to write this book. Thank you from the bottom of my heart. I hope each one of you buys a copy of the book for yourself and a few for your friends. And then I hope you invite me to speak to your group. It's much better in person!

Table of Contents

FOREWORD

By Ed Grisamore

I didn't laugh the first time I heard Bruce Goddard speak. I howled. My sides split. My eyes watered. I learned never to be chewing on your casserole when Bruce is telling one of his funny stories. Your neighbors won't appreciate it when you can't control the food coming out of your nose.

It was in the spring of 1997 at a civic club meeting in Macon. Afterward, I flagged down Bruce in the parking lot, introduced myself, and told him we really ought to get together.

It wasn't long before I found myself rocking on the front porch at Goddard Funeral Home in Reynolds. There, Bruce did it again. Got me laughing. Kept me laughing.

It has been eight years now, and I haven't stopped laughing. In many ways, Bruce and I have become like brothers. We are kindred spirits. We are both story-tellers. We do a lot of public speaking because of our jobs. We are rabid Georgia Bulldogs and take delight in the simple pleasures of life.

We were raised by wonderful parents who provided us with a firm foundation. They made sure our bottoms were in the pew every Sunday morning. We both married remarkable women. We are both blessed with three wonderful sons. And we both found our calling in life. Some might call it a job, a career, an avocation. We consider it a ministry.

When Bruce tells his stories about being a fourth-generation undertaker from a small Georgia town, he is not laughing in the face of death. He is celebrating life, with all its quirky imperfections.

"I laugh a lot and enjoy life, but I honestly think I'm also very sensitive to what people are going through," Bruce once told me. "And my messages reinforce themselves."

He makes us think. He makes us smile. He knows how to widen those smiles into laughter. In peeling back the layers and helping us understand and appreciate the lighter side of dying, he has no doubt saved lives, too. After all, the Bible tells us laughter is tonic for the soul, the best prescription on the market for happiness. Bruce always points to Proverbs 17:22. "A cheerful heart is good medicine, but a crushed spirit dries up the bones."

For several years, I've joined the chorus of people who have encouraged Bruce to compile his stories in a book. Now those stories have come to life in a new way. You hold in your hands a true gift. Laugh. Cry. Remember. If you do laugh – and you will – just put down your fork. Don't touch that casserole.

Ed Grisamore
Columnist, *Macon Telegraph*
Author of *Smack Dab in Dog Crossing*

THE PROLOGUE

"I would guess there are not a whole lot of under-taker/humorists running around the country."

I am a fourth generation undertaker from Reynolds, Georgia. My brother was an undertaker, my Daddy was an undertaker, my granddaddy was an undertaker, and my great-granddaddy was an undertaker. I was born to be an undertaker.

I don't know how much you know about "undertaking," but let me tell something about making a living being an undertaker. It is an honorable profession. It also can be a very difficult profession. As a kid, I watched my dad walk into some of the toughest situations this life has to offer and immediately make things better. Daddy had a God-given gift to do that and he used his gift as well as anyone I've ever seen. Because of what I saw, I wanted to grow up to be a person who had the ability and opportunity to make things better for others in the difficult times of life. I think his gift became my gift. At least I like to think that is true.

I am also a humorist and motivational speaker. I really never aspired to be a humorist and motivational speaker. I would guess there are not a whole lot of undertaker/humorists running around the country. Don't know how it happened. I guess I just backed into it.

Actually, when I think about it, I suppose there is at least one reason I started this "second profession." It has to do with the population of Reynolds. The truth is there are just not a whole lot of folks who live in Reynolds, and that means there are not a lot of folks who die there. I had to do something to make a living.

When you think about it, it is amazing how long it

seems people live when you are in my kind of business. I always tell the story about my friend Tom, who went to the doctor to get his "sixty-year-old physical." After the doctor had checked him out, he told him to go in his office and wait for him. Of course, that scared Tom half to death. You know how it is when the doctor checks you out and then says he wants to talk to you. Finally, the doctor came in and told Tom that he could not believe how healthy he was and asked him what he did to stay so healthy. Tom replied that he exercised. "I walk in the morning, walk in the afternoon, play golf three times a week – and I even go snow skiing twice a year."

The doctor said, "Whatever you are doing is working. I just don't see too many sixty–year-olds that are in as good of shape as you are."

Then the doctor asked another probing question, "How old was your Daddy when he died?"

Tom abruptly responded, "Did I say my Daddy was dead?"

The doctor replied, "My goodness, I just assumed your dad was dead since you are sixty years old."

"No," Tom said, "he's in good shape too! He exercises everyday, walks in the morning, walks in the afternoon, and plays golf every single day of his life."

"That is amazing," the doctor quizzically replied. "Now that I think about it, I guess long life just kind of runs in your family."

"How old was your grandfather when he died?" the doctor then asked.

"Did I say my grandfather was dead?" Tom quickly replied.

"My gosh, Tom! He must be a hundred years old!"

Tom replied, "Doc, as a matter of fact he is 106! He exercises every day too. He is in great shape. Doc, you won't believe this, but he's fixing to get married!"

Now astonished, the doctor asked, "Why in the world would a 106-year-old man want to get married?"

Tom had him now. "Did I say he *wanted* to get married?"

Now maybe you understand better. People do live a long time these days – and Reynolds didn't have many residents – so I had to do something to make a living. So I started speaking – for pay.

It still amazes me how many invitations I get to speak. I have spoken to every group you can imagine: from civic clubs to national conventions, from church groups to a room full of drunks, from family night suppers to sales rallies, from nursing homes to corporate America.

I never did any marketing for these speaking engagements. I just speak one place and someone from that crowd asks me to speak at the next place.

It finally dawned on me that if that many people are asking me to speak, they must like what I am saying, so I decided I ought to write this book. Never written a book, mind you, but I had never spoken publicly until I stood in front of a crowd one day.

What you are about to read is a story of an ordinary guy who grew up in a small town and who was blessed to have a very unique perspective on life. It includes humorous stories about a subject most don't like to talk about. But I hope you will find much more in the pages of this book.

It is a story about life at its very best. It is a story about incredible parents, incredible family, incredible people, and an incredible community. It is also a story about an incredible profession.

But more than anything, it is a story of an incredible God who has proven himself over and over to us all.

Chapter One

LIFE IN REYNOLDS, GEORGIA

"In 1866, my great-grandfather moved from Macon, Georgia, to Reynolds, Georgia, to start a business. He did that because he thought Reynolds was on the verge of becoming a booming city."

It Was a Conspiracy

I was born in Reynolds, Georgia. Reynolds is a very small town located in Taylor County, which is in the middle part of the state, about halfway between Macon and Columbus. I would not take a million dollars for being born and raised in Reynolds, Georgia.

The friendships and relationships that I have established in that little town have carried me in life. The greatest people in the world live in Reynolds, Georgia.

Make no mistake; Reynolds is very small in population and physical size. "Welcome to Reynolds" and "Hurry Back" could have been on the same sign. But in my mind and in my heart and when I look back on my life, Reynolds was very big. It was big because of the special people who lived there. And it was big because of how those special people influenced my life.

Everybody who was raised in Reynolds in those days was raised by the whole town. If you got a spanking at school, you would get a whooping when you got home. There is a difference between a spanking and a whooping. It was not unusual to get a whooping by your buddy's Mama either. If not, she would surely call your Mama when you did something wrong, and your Mama would be waiting at the door to tend to you when you got home. A little boy just couldn't get by being bad in Reynolds.

I remember the time I ordered a certain forbidden

magazine that was published by a nudist colony. I'm not sure how I found out how to order such a magazine, but I did. It clearly stated the magazine would come in the mail disguised in brown paper. It did come wrapped in brown paper, but it did not fool Blanche, our local postmaster. Blanche personally delivered the magazine to my Mama at our house. I came in from playing late one afternoon, and there she was sitting in the living room, showing Mama what I had ordered. Mama did not take too kindly to the revelation that I had ordered such a magazine. I won't tell you how I was disciplined for that (I can tell you that "time out" was not in Mama's vocabulary), but I will tell you I never ordered anything by mail again unless I knew that Blanche would approve.

This continued even to my college years. When I was in college, I used to cash checks three or four times a week at Five Points Beer & Wine. I never had any cash with me in college and the guy that ran the place was a fraternity brother. It was just convenient to cash checks there. Somehow I was not surprised when Mama called me one day and began asking me questions about my alcohol consumption. After several minutes of interrogation, she finally told me that her friend at the bank (who happened to be my Sunday school teacher) had called and said I was spending all my money on beer and wine. Now that is a full service bank!

But this little town did pretty well at raising kids. It has always amazed me at how many people who grew up in Reynolds turned out to be very successful in life. I think there are more doctors, lawyers, teachers, ministers, and business leaders from Reynolds as a percentage of population than any town anywhere. I can't prove that, but it would be interesting to do a little research to confirm it.

I think there are a few reasons for that, not the least of which had to do with the quality of our school. Mr. Joiner, the longtime principal, ruled the school with an iron hand. Receiving an education was not optional under his administration. I've never met anyone who was a student in Reynolds under Mr. Joiner who did not have the highest regard for him. In fact, around Reynolds there were three great influencers of people: God, Jesus Christ, and Mr. Joiner. I never was clear on the order of importance, but they were all way up there. After he retired there was a huge picture of him that hung in the hall at the high school. When you walked by and looked at his likeness hanging on the wall, his eyes would follow you. It was like he was still watching over the place. Mr. Joiner probably positively influenced more people than any other person Reynolds ever produced. Mr. Joiner retired about the time I started the first grade, so I never got to be under his tutelage directly. But I was definitely under his influence because all of my teachers were his protégés. And the schoolteachers in Reynolds were the best of the best.

The teachers we had did much more than teach reading, writing, and arithmetic. The older I get, the more I realize how well they did that. But they did much more. They invested their lives in the kids that sat in their classrooms, and they did that over a very long period of time. My first teacher was Mrs. Crawley who was one of my Mama's close friends. She was the wife of a local attorney and was the mother of four children. Mrs. Crawley started a kindergarten in a little building they had built in their yard for that purpose. When I was five years old, I attended that kindergarten with many of the group of classmates I would continue on with in grade school and have close relationships the rest of my life.

Two of Mrs. Crawley's own children were in that class and continue to be in that group of life long friends. Mike and Will Crawley (later known as "Big Hip and Little Hip") were identical twins, and when they were young, they could put away some food with the best of them. They were the only people I have ever known who got banned for life from a catfish restaurant. Until they finally got caught, they would enter a nearby "all you can eat" catfish restaurant wearing the same color shirt. "Big Hip" would go in the restroom while "Little Hip" sat at the table to eat. After a few minutes of serious eating, they would swap places. In other words they would get two very large meals for the price of one. I am not sure how they figured out how to do that, but I am sure they did *not* learn it from the lessons their mom taught us in kindergarten.

Many of our elementary school teachers also taught our parents. They were also our aunts, grandmothers, and Sunday school teachers. They knew everything about us before we ever sat in the desk in their room, and there was no way you could pull the wool over their eyes. They made you learn, and they were very good at it too. They also disciplined you when it was necessary, and you would get disciplined again when you got home. In today's educational environment, if a child gets disciplined at school (which is not often) the parents will, at the least, demand a meeting with the principal. Some will even file a lawsuit. It was different growing up in Reynolds. The teachers and the parents were part of a conspiracy, but it was a conspiracy I am very thankful for today.

To illustrate, I remember the last day of school when I was finishing the third grade. Summer break had come! This was always the most exciting day of the year, and they usually let us out early. Waiting on that last bell, everyone would be leaning in the start position as if the gun were about to sound beginning a 100 yard dash. After the bell sounded, and everybody took off for the summer, my friend Chuck and I decided we would play a cruel joke on our classmate Robert. We grabbed him and put him in the back of the new city garbage truck that was parked at the school. Mama Byrd, who was our third-grade teacher and also happened to be Chuck's grandmother, witnessed our foolishness. She came out, grabbed us both by the arm, took us back into the school building and made us stay after school. This was the last day of school, mind you, and everyone had gone home but us. But we had to sit there. I do believe that was the most difficult punishment I ever received. I was not at all surprised that Mama already knew about what I had done when I finally got home and so did Chuck's mom. We both got an old-fashioned family whooping, and we both had to go to Robert's house to apologize. Our summer got off to a rough start. But I never helped put anyone in the garbage truck again.

One of the neatest things about Fridays during the school year was that there was a good possibility you would get to invite someone to spend the night with you. Or better than that, you would get invited to spend the night with someone else. All that depended on whether or not you were in trouble. The parents definitely used the "spend the night" parties as leverage. As I said, it was a conspiracy and all the parents were in on it.

I'll never forget the first time I spent the night away from home. I spent half a day packing a huge suitcase. You would think I was going to camp for the summer. I had been invited to spend the night at Alan Whatley's, which was just two doors down from our house. Alan was much more independent than me and had spent the night with me many times, but up to then, I hadn't got up the nerve to spend the night with him. I was ready. I walked down to their house with my huge suitcase, and within five minutes I was homesick and wanted to come home. You would have thought I was 500 miles away. In reality, I could throw a rock and hit our house. But I came back home. I eventually spent the night with Alan many times. They later moved out in the country, and Alan and I spent a lot of time exploring the chicken houses and the woods behind their house. At the Whatleys' there was a refreshment time at 3:30 p.m. I couldn't figure out why we couldn't eat junk there like we did at our house. At my house we ate snacks whenever we wanted as long as we could find something to eat. Today I realize the Whatleys' refreshment time was for our own good. It was a conspiracy, I tell you. They were all in it together. And every time I see Alan's mom, "Miss" Hazel, I stop, and we hug, and she knows and I know that she had a lot to do with whoever I am.

I used to love to spend the night with Stan at the Montgomery farm in the Crowell community. They had what seemed like miles of woods to explore and did we ever more explore it. Stan's mom, "Miss" Mary, made the best hamburgers I had ever eaten. She let us do all kinds of stuff. Stan and I slept in a wagon full of cotton one Friday night. I thought I had gone to heaven. I learned a lot about life spending the night at the Montgomerys' on that farm. Today whenever I run into "Miss" Mary, I hug her too. She has that familiar twinkle in her eye, as if to say, "I helped raise you." And she did.

The Byrds' house was another fun place to go. Chuck, who was my partner in the garbage-truck incident, was one of my best buddies. His dad was a renowned trial lawyer and also happened to be the Lieutenant Governor of Georgia. He was later the front runner in the race for governor but had a heart attack and had to withdraw from the race, (I told you Reynolds produced some successful people.) Chuck's older brother, Buster, was quite a character. Buster created a nickname for almost everybody in Reynolds. He named me "Lucy" and named Chuck "Woochie." And everybody in Reynolds called us by those names!

My buddies Billy Bell and Eddie Ayers had birthdays the same day (or maybe a day apart). Their moms, "Miss" Frances and "Miss" Mary, decided to have a joint birthday party on a certain birthday, and they planned a big one. We were all going to Columbus to appear on the *Cap-O-Hap* TV show. Everybody in Reynolds had their TV antennas pointing towards Columbus so they could see the Reynolds kids on television. This was a huge day for Reynolds! Chuck and I were standing in line on live TV with all the other kids to speak to Cap-O-Hap himself. The routine was, when it came our time, he would ask each of us to speak into the microphone while looking at the camera and give our names. All the parents, including the Lieutenant Governor and his wife, were watching anxiously to see their kid appear and speak on TV. Chuck and I decided we would make Buster proud (and embarrass our parents) by introducing ourselves with our nicknames instead of our real names. Chuck would introduce himself as "Woochie Byrd" and I would introduce myself as "Lucy Goddard." We had it all planned.

Chuck went first and with the confidence of a lawyer (he would later become one) looked straight into the camera and said, "I'm Woochie Byrd from Reynolds, Georgia." I followed right after him and spoke with the compassion of an undertaker (I later became one), "I'm Bruce Goddard from Reynolds, Georgia." To this day, Chuck thinks I set him up. The truth is I chickened out. He got scolded by every parent in Reynolds when we got back to town. It was a conspiracy, I tell you.

Chuck and I discovered at one point in our elementary school journey that we were going with the same girl. Imagine that! When you think about it, it is not surprising we had the same girlfriend. Chuck was related to most of the girls our age in our school. There was just not that many for him to choose from. I should have backed off and allowed Chuck to have one of the few girls in school who was not a branch off his family tree. Chuck's mom, "Miss" Gloria, decided she would help us out and suggested we go in together to get Vicki a birthday present. That sounded good to us because we knew we could save a little money. So with the help of "Miss" Gloria, we purchased a little red suitcase from Windham's Dime Store. On the card we wrote, "Dear Vicki, Happy Birthday. We love you, Woochie and Lucy." After I became an adult, I hardly ever saw "Miss" Gloria when she did not laugh and remind me of the story about the little red suitcase. As I look back I realize that she was teaching both of us how to turn lemons into lemonade – and to smile in the process.

Jimmy Childre, Jr. was another of my best friends. He spent many nights at my house and I spent many nights at his house. Jimmy and I were christened together as babies, were best friends in high school, and today remain very close friends. His folks were in the car business, and his grandfather Swearingen would hide the new Chevrolets in his back yard to keep people from seeing them until the day came for them to be unveiled. Jimmy would always take a few of us over to Mr. Swearingen's house to preview the new cars before anyone else saw them. It was an annual event, and nobody wanted Jimmy to be mad with them in the fall because they didn't want to be left out of this event. Today, parents fly their kids to Disney World once a year and spend tons of money to be entertained. The kids know the trip is coming and look forward to it for months. We were entertained just fine in the back yard of Mr. Swearingen's house. We looked forward to that day every fall. And it didn't cost our parents a red cent.

Jimmy and I spent most of our childhood days on the Reynolds Golf Course. We got pretty good at golf too. If I had a dollar for every round of golf I played with Jimmy, I could retire. We both later went to high school in nearby Fort Valley because the school in Reynolds was consolidated with the school in Butler. We were pretty much inseparable in high school, and we both made the golf team as ninth graders at the much larger high school. The first day we went to school in Fort Valley, they had class elections. We were brand new and hardly knew anybody there. I couldn't believe it when Jimmy was voted the freshman class president and I was elected to escort Patty Wilson, the ninth-grade representative, in the Miss Vallihi Beauty Pageant. We laughed all the way home. Jimmy eventually would own his own car dealership and would become a very successful and well-known business leader. He has studied at Harvard Business School, received a MBA from Duke University, and studied extensively throughout the world. He even gave the commencement address for his graduation from Duke. It all started for him in Reynolds and he will tell you today he gives much of the credit to the people of that little town who raised him there.

The James family lived next door to us. They had two good-looking daughters, Jenny and Marsha. I learned how to play basketball on their goal in their back yard. There is no telling how many hours Marsha and I played "horse" and "poison" and "one on one" basketball in their yard with that old crooked rim and wooden backboard. Later, Marsha and I went to Fort Valley to high school, and we both became the leading scorers on our teams. I remember sitting in the stands with great pride, watching Marsha play basketball. I knew every move she would make, and I was her greatest cheerleader. And she was mine. Sometimes we would catch each other's eye when one of us was playing and the other was watching. We worked many hours together to learn to play this game, and we were reaping the dividends for all our hard work and all the fun we had. I don't get to see Marsha much anymore. We have always exchanged Christmas cards. But when we do see each other we stop, and we hug, and we are reminded of how our lives are so closely linked. We are family. We were raised next door to each other. We spent much of our childhood together, and we were raised by that little town we call Reynolds.

Right across the street from us was another set of Whatleys, as in the Julian and Sue variety. They were like my second parents. They had two good-looking daughters, too, and they also had a swimming pool. No wonder my hormones were always raging! Debbie was a year older than me, and Donna (we called her Tuggie) was four years younger. Debbie was my first girlfriend. When I was growing up I always figured I would marry either Debbie or Tuggie – really didn't matter which one either. I now realize that would have been kind of like marrying your sister. Their backyard pool was the gathering place in Reynolds for many years for all the boys on the prowl. I can tell you, it was great hunting! One of the highlights of my summer was to get to rub suntan oil on the backs of the cute girls that hung around the pool. Sue saw me helping one of the girls out with her tan one day and told me I couldn't do that anymore. That was one of the saddest days of my life. I'm telling you there was a conspiracy and all the parents were in on it.

I'll never forget the day Daddy died, many years later. I was 39 years old. A lot of years had passed since we were all running around that neighborhood as kids. I found myself at that home that brought back so many wonderful memories. I was attempting to get myself together so I could greet the crowd of people who were coming to visit. I looked up and Debbie was standing in the kitchen. She lived in Atlanta (two hours away) and as soon as she got word of Daddy's death, she dropped everything and headed straight to Reynolds. I had done pretty well up until then. When I saw her, we grabbed each other and we hugged each other and held on, and we wept. You see, my parents were like her parents, and her parents were like mine. We are more than friends; we are family; and we will be forever linked.

Our other next door neighbors were another set of Whatleys. This was Dr. Whatley and Rosemary. They had *three* good looking daughters: Linda, Nancy and Suzy. (As I write this, it is becoming very clear to me that I have always been surrounded by two groups of people: Whatleys and good looking women.) Dr. Whatley and Rosemary also had a son, Jimmy, who later would be known as Jim. Jim and his youngest sister, Suzy, both followed in their dad's footsteps and became doctors.

After my junior year in high school I started dating

Kathy Underwood, who lived on the outskirts of town. Lynn, Kathy's older sister, had recently broken up with a boyfriend, and I told Jim she needed consoling. So Jim and Lynn double dated with Kathy and me the next weekend. Three years later, Jim and Lynn were married. Three years after that, Kathy and I were married. So my next door neighbor became my brother-in-law. Just for the record, Mrs. Underwood also had some good-looking daughters.

Our back yard and Dr. Whatley's back yard were connected, and this was where all the kids in the neighborhood and from other parts of town played baseball. It was also the local golf driving range. I cannot even begin to tell you how many windows we knocked out with baseballs and golf balls in those two back yards.

I hope I'm painting you a picture here. The James' house next door was where we played basketball. We swam and frolicked in the swimming pool across the street at Julian and Sue's house. And we played baseball and practiced golf in the back yards of our house and Dr. Whatley's house. And we ate wherever there was food. Wherever we were, those particular Mamas were in charge. And they had free reign to encourage, rebuke, and discipline each other's children. It was a conspiracy. They were all in it together. But I now realize how well they did it and how fortunate we all were.

I think there was another reason Reynolds was so unique. It had to do with "community." Life revolved around the church, the school, and civic activities. There were no bars, night clubs, or beer stores in

Reynolds. Those that did "take a drink" on a Saturday night would have to go out of town to buy it and sneak it back in town inconspicuously in a brown bag. And they would drink mouthwash afterwards so nobody could smell it on them in Sunday school the next morning. When the Kiwanis Club had a pancake supper, everybody in town attended. When the school had a basketball game or a track meet, everybody in town was there to cheer them on. When the church doors were open, everybody was there. When the Baptist church had a revival, the Methodist church would cancel their services to attend, and the Baptists would do the same for the Methodists. Everybody did everything together, and everybody had lifelong relationships with each other.

And the community was made up of people from all walks of life. Most people today hang around people who are just like themselves. We live in neighborhoods where everyone is close to being on the same step of the economic ladder. We attend churches and Sunday school classes and social events where we find people who are like us. That was not the case growing up in Reynolds. People from different economic and social positions in life joined together to form a community. All the community was family, no matter which side of the tracks they came from or what kind of house they lived in or what kind of car they drove.

I saw that very clearly a few years ago when my eighth-grade Reynolds elementary class had a class reunion after some 35 years. Almost everybody in our old Reynolds class showed up. An outsider looking in at the reunion celebration would wonder how in the world that group would have enough in common to even have conversations much less a celebration. The truth is we had everything in common. It had nothing to do with how much money we made or anyone's social success.

We had Reynolds in common. We were all raised by that little town. And we have been, and we will be, friends forever.

The Simple Life

The downtown section of Reynolds consisted of two streets that intersected each other. There were many little stores and the owners made good livings. People did not go out of town to shop in those days, and everyone supported the merchants and the town. Later, when the mega stores in larger towns came into existence, people started going to those stores to shop, and the little town as we knew it would never be the same.

But when Reynolds was in its prime, it was a busy place and there was a variety of stores. A shopper had no reason to go out of town to shop because he could pretty much buy whatever he needed right there. There were two full-service grocery stores, four gas stations, several smaller general stores, a bank, a fish market, three clothing stores, a hardware store, a dime store, an appliance store, several farm-supply warehouses, a dry cleaners, a flower shop, an automobile dealership, a bank, a phone company, two barber shops, a couple of beauty parlors, a few cotton gins, and a rural electric cooperative. All those businesses were located on two streets that made up downtown Reynolds. Saturday was always the busiest day of the week. Everybody came to town on Saturday.

Mr. Hicks Trussell's store was the neatest to me. He sold canned goods and stuff, but he also had a little counter with stools for customers, and he cooked hamburgers behind it. He kept hamburger meat rolled into little balls in his refrigerator. When you ordered a hamburger, he would take out a little ball of hamburger meat, throw it on his skillet, flatten it out, and start cooking. I was sitting there one afternoon waiting on a hamburger I had ordered when Eulan Brown sat down next to me. Eulan rode a bicycle everywhere he went and delivered *Grit* newspapers for a living. He also had a physical handicap and it was not unusual to see his bicycle lying on its side on one of the Reynolds streets with *Grit* papers strewn everywhere. You would see Eulan trying to pick himself up, gather the papers together, and start over again. I joined many other kids in town and laughed at his clumsiness. We never got too close to Eulan because he was a little scary to us. But that day I sat on the stool next to him at Trussell's Store and talked to him for the first time. I saw him as a human being and in a completely differ-ent light. I never laughed at Eulan's infirmity again after that. I was beginning to learn a very important principle of life that would become much clearer as I grew older. I would later discover that there would be times when I would fall on my face and have to pick myself up, gather together what I had strewn, and start over again. I can tell you that I never forgot Eulan Brown.

Mr. E. T. Shealy also had an interesting little store. Mr. Shealy was a quiet, churchgoing man like most of the other merchants in town, but he had a separate "shady" business he operated in the back of his store. Many of the Reynolds boys would go to Mr. Shealy to get their warts removed. I'm not sure what he did to get rid of the warts because I never got up the nerve to visit him. He would take them in the back and do some hocus pocus stuff and the warts would fall off in a few days. Mr. Shealy's greatest accomplishment, though, would be giving Charlie Hicks his start in life. Charlie worked for Mr. Shealy as a boy, and Mr. Shealy gave him responsibility that was uncommon in those days. Charlie Hicks would become a very successful businessman and one of the most well-known African-American business and civic leaders in the state of Georgia. He got his start at E. T. Shealy's store in downtown Reynolds.

Mr. W. M. Hollis had a store in Reynolds for a while when I was growing up. It was located in the old post office. He repaired shoes and piddled with whatever came his way. I think he was in his retirement years and was just doing that to have something to do. He was sitting in a chair in the front of his store one afternoon cleaning his pistol when it accidentally fired. Bill Hawkins happened to be walking by, and the bullet hit Bill in the foot. Bill was not hurt badly, but he was always convinced that Mr. Hollis was shooting at him that day on purpose. After that incident, anytime Bill would see Mr. Hollis coming, he would go the other way. He was scared to death of him. When you met Bill Hawkins on the street he would always ask you this question: "How many Griggs are there?" He would answer himself, "Six boys and four girls." Then he would ask, "Do they *drank*?" And he would answer himself again, "They ain't dead, are they?" And then his last statement would always be this: "Mr. W. M. Hollis – he'll shoot you, won't he?"

Brady's store was where we bought our clothes. George and Cat Brady owned that store and they were our neighbors and close friends. If Mama happened to buy a shirt for me from an out-of-town store (which was rare), Cat would notice it and ask me where she got it. The truth is, the merchants in Reynolds held each other accountable to shop locally and support each other. They all had earned the right to ask those kinds of questions. When I was a very young boy, George died suddenly of a heart attack late one after- noon after cutting his grass. Cat and their daughter, Caroline, were left to fend for themselves. I remem- ber his sudden death affected me greatly as a young kid, and it also affected my Daddy. That was the first time I saw my Daddy cry. Cat continued to run Brady's store alone for many more years until her retirement. Some years after George died, Hazel Lane began working with Cat at Brady's. Hazel would eventually buy the store from Cat and run her own store. Hazel was one of the most determined people I ever knew. When she was a child, she fell in a fire, and as a result, her hands were burned and were essentially nonex- istent. She overcame her handicap and could do anything anybody else could do, including play golf. She and Cat were avid golfers. Hazel had a way to strap the club on her wrist, and she was a very good golfer.

Some of the ladies in Reynolds went on a shop- ping trip to Atlanta one day. Hazel was among them, and she purchased a new dress. The other ladies picked out a pair of gloves for Hazel that would go with her new dress. When they realized what they had done (Hazel had no hands), they were totally embarrassed until Hazel explained that their act was the nicest thing anyone had done for her. This proved to her that her friends did not even think of her as handicapped. Hazel was always a role model for me. She played with the cards she had been dealt and overcame the obstacles in her path. I learned a lot about life watching Hazel Lane live her life.

All the businesses in Reynolds closed every Thursday at noon. That's the day all the merchants took the afternoon off to go fishing or to play golf. And they closed promptly at noon. My brothers and I spent more Thursday afternoons than I could ever possibly remember playing golf with our dad. As I look back, those were the most fun times I had in life. We were not working – we were just together and having fun. I know he could have easily spent that afternoon off with his friends – without his kids. But he chose to spend it with us. On most days his friends joined us and our friends did as well, but we were always there and very much a part of his life.

Reynolds Pharmacy, owned and operated by another Whatley (Leonard), was the afternoon hangout for all the kids in Reynolds. The attraction was the soda fountain. Most of the kids would come by after school, sit on a stool, and hang out at that soda fountain. They made real milkshakes and real cherry cokes. Later, much to the dismay of all the kids, Leonard closed the soda fountain, and the kids had no reason to hang out there anymore. Then the pharmacy became the morning hangout for the older people. All the old geezers gathered there in the morning to drink coffee and chew the fat and enjoy life. Leonard had purchased the drug store many years earlier from his Uncle Clay.

Sid James and his wife, Eula Maude, lived about two miles outside of Reynolds off Highway 96 towards Fort Valley. One morning back when Leonard's Uncle Clay was running the drug store, Sid woke up with a bad case of the itch, and he knew he had to do something about it. Now, it was the kind of itch that you are not supposed to talk about in a public place, but he had it and I'm about to tell you about it.

And you know the kind of itch I'm talking about.

Sid frantically drove down to the drug store, walked in, and proclaimed for whoever was there to hear, "Clay, I've got a bad case of the itch. I can't sleep at night, and I'm keeping Eula Maude up too. You've got to give me something!"

Clay went in the back of his store, mixed Sid a concoction, and poured it in a little medicine bottle. He walked out front and said, "Sid, I know you can be hardheaded, but you need to listen to me. You need to go home and fill your bathtub up with cool water. Right before you sit in the tub, you should just dab this stuff on you."

"Sid, this stuff is *hot*!" Then he said, "A little dab will do you!"

Sid thanked him and drove back out to his house and went straight to the bathroom. He went in the bathroom, closed the door, and filled the tub with cool water. He took his clothes off and did exactly what

Clay had told him to do. He dabbed a little on him.

But before he got in the tub he stood there a minute and thought, "If a little bit of this stuff will help me, I believe the whole bottle should help more!" So, he emptied the contents of the bottle of Clay's concoction and rubbed it in real good. Then he sat in the tub.

In just a few minutes, he yelled as loud as he could, "Eula Maude!"

Eula Maude came to the door and asked Sid what in the world was the matter.

"Eula Maude," he cried, "Go get the car!"

"Sid, what in the world are you doing? Are you in the tub?"

"Eula Maude, for one time in your life, please do what I'm asking you to do! Just go outside, get in the car, and drive it to the back door. When you get there, honk the horn!"

Eula Maude did as he told her to do. She drove the car to the back door and honked the horn.

Sid jumped out of the tub buck-naked, ran out of the bathroom, down the hall, and outside the door. He then jumped on the hood of the car, pulled both legs back, and yelled at the top of his lungs, "Drive, woman, drive!!"

I think hood ornaments were invented in Reynolds. Can you imagine riding down the road and meeting that car with Sid on the hood?

There was also a hospital right in the middle of town. The two doctors were not only charged with taking care of the sick, but they were surgeons too and also delivered most of the babies that came along. I was one of those babies. I was born at Sams-Whatley

Hospital on September 20, 1954. The doctor who delivered me was our next-door neighbor. Remember, we played baseball and golf in his back yard.

Dr. Sams and Dr. Whatley owned the hospital, and they never slept. On second thought, I guess they had to sleep some, but I can tell you they lived on much less sleep than everyone else. They worked all day at the hospital seeing patients or performing surgery or delivering babies – and at night they made house calls. If you had a cold or a pain, you would just call the hospital and get on their list. One of the two doctors would eventually stop by your house later in the night with his little black bag, check you out, and give you a shot or whatever else you needed. They spoiled the heck out of the people of Reynolds. If it was in the daytime, you would just go to the hospital and sit in the waiting room and wait for your name to be called. Then you would be escorted into one of the examining rooms. A few close friends would call ahead and ask the nurses to slip them in the back door and into an examining room so they wouldn't have to wait in the waiting room. That was one reason it was not unusual for a person to sit all day in the waiting room to see the doctor – others were always breaking in line through the back door. I am sure of this: There was no such thing as a doctor's appointment in Reynolds.

The story was told about an examination Dr. Sams was attempting on Mr. McDaniel that really stirred up everyone in the waiting room one morning. Mr. McDaniel was suffering from a severe stomachache, and someone in the waiting room let him go ahead so he could see a doctor. Dr. Sams asked Mr. McDaniel to remove his clothes and lie down on the examining table. After doing a little checking and feeling around, Dr. Sams asked Mr. McDaniel to roll over on his side and bend his knees. Dr. Sams grabbed the KY Jelly and proceeded to put on his rubber examining gloves. He was about to begin the examination when Mr. McDaniel suddenly jumped up, turned around, and screamed at the top of his lungs, "My gosh, Doc! Watch what you are doing! You almost stuck your finger in my fanny!" Everybody in the waiting room cringed.

I remember being a patient in that hospital on several different occasions. The ladies in the church would usually visit the church members when they were in the hospital. Mrs. Sawyer, who attended our church, was also the local Avon lady. She would always be one of the first to visit, and she would always bring a bottle of Avon cologne as a gift if you were really sick. Whenever I got sick, I would always ask Mama to be sure to call Mrs. Sawyer and let her know how bad I was doing.

Most kids started driving in Reynolds when they turned fifteen. Sixteen was the legal age, but the police would look the other way. I think they figured that the 15-year-olds that drove couldn't be worse than the old timers who were driving the streets. Driving in Reynolds was like driving in a combat zone. There were a few old people, my grandfather being one of them, who had no regard for stop signs. I learned that the hard way. I was 16 years old and driving down Macon Street in my 1964 push-button Plymouth when Mr. Eric Newsom pulled out in front of me at an intersection in his pickup truck. I swerved to miss him and ended up in the Cook's back yard. It didn't bother Mr. Newsom one bit either. He looked at me over in the bushes like what in the world are you doing, and he just kept going.

My dad and I watched my grandfather run a stop sign in the middle of town one day when a woman broadsided him. We ran out to be sure he and the woman were okay. My grandfather jumped out of the car and proceeded to bless the lady out. Daddy tried to explain to his dad that he had run the stop sign and it was his fault. My grandfather replied, "Son, I was riding these roads before they had stop signs!"

Years later, my Daddy drove just like his Daddy. He backed into me three times in one day, and each time he said it was my fault.

Reynolds had two policemen when I was growing up. The chief was L. D. Gordon, and he ran things during the day. William Wainwright was the night policeman. Mr. William's job was to walk through the town at night and check the doors of all the businesses to be sure they were locked. After he got through making his rounds, he would sit in a chair in front of the city hall, tilt his police cap over his eyes, lean his chair back, and doze off. On many nights, Donald Powell, one of my classmates, would slip out of the upstairs window of his house in the middle of the night, slide down the TV antenna pole, and ride his bicycle up to the city hall and sit with Mr. William the rest of the night. We always knew at school when Donald had been up with Mr. William the night before. He would lay his head on his desk and fall asleep. Donald would eventually become the Reynolds Postmaster.

I actually visited Mr. William at the city hall on a few occasions myself. Mr. William taught me an interesting lesson one night. He explained to me in great detail that there was no need to kill a mosquito after he bit you. He said that once a mosquito bites you he will die anyway. I have no idea if that is true, but he sure was convincing to a young boy. But I never had enough willpower to just watch the mosquito after he had bit. I always continued to slap him anyway. Mr. William was a very easygoing man who loved to spend time with us kids. Years later, when I was in Athens, Georgia, in college, I turned the radio on one Saturday morning and heard a news bulletin that a policeman had been shot in Reynolds. I pulled off to the side of the road. Mr. William had heard some noise in the business across the street from the city hall in the middle of the night, walked over to check it out, and surprised some burglars. He chased them across town, and they shot him and killed him in the alley behind the hospital. I couldn't imagine what kind of jerk would have the nerve to kill Mr. William Wainwright – still makes me sick at my stomach.

Reynolds also had two barber shops in town. There was Jim Brewer's Sanitary Barber Shop and Hill's Barber Shop that was across the street. I often wondered if Mr. Jim was saying that his shop was sanitary and Hill's was dirty. Mr. Jim (at the sanitary barber shop) cut my hair. I always thought I got my hair cut there because Mr. Jim was Methodist. Wayne Hill was Baptist, so I suppose he handled the Baptist hair. There were always people hanging out at both barber shops. Either of these places was the place to be if one wanted to catch up on the local news.

I was in Mr. Jim's shop one day to get my hair cut during the height of the Beatles' popularity. Eddie Ayers was there to get his hair cut and was ahead of me. Eddie had a "crew cut," which means his hair was very short. When Mr. Jim would get through with a customer, he would always yell, "Next!" Whoever was up better be ready to go or he would miss his turn. Eddie was ready this day, and he quickly jumped in the chair when his time came. Mr. Jim asked the usual question, "How you want it?" Eddie responded that he wanted a "Beatle" haircut. I was sitting there wondering how in the world Mr. Jim was going to do that. I didn't think he knew who the Beatles were, much less how to cut a Beatle haircut. Either way, with Eddie's short hair, I knew Mr. Jim's only hope was a wig.

I'll never forget the day I decided to go over to Wayne Hill's barber shop to get a haircut. Mr. Jim had gotten pretty old and he would cut you with those barber clippers of his. He kept band-aids handy, and that helped, but two band-aids for one haircut was a little much for a growing boy, so I decided to go to Hill's. I was sitting in the chair halfway through my haircut, when the door opened and there stood Mr. Jim. He looked at me like I had committed a terrible sin. I stared at the floor knowing I had betrayed him. I felt terrible.

Reynolds had two full-service grocery stores. The Aultmans owned one of them and the Goddards owned the other. This is where my memories of growing up in Reynolds get really personal. I spent my entire childhood working at Goddard's store. I started by sacking up groceries, moved up to the produce counter, advanced on to the meat market, and finally proved myself enough for my dad to let me handle the money.

The Aultmans had their customers and we had our customers and both families made a living, but there was plenty of competition between the two. When I think about it, it was difficult for the people in Reynolds to know where to shop because the people were friends with both families. I remember Sams-Whatley hospital had a kitchen and staff who cooked home-cooked meals for the patients in the hospital. The hospital bought groceries from Goddard's Store one year and Aultman's Store the next year to be fair, but more likely, to keep the peace. But like the Aultmans, we wanted all the business we could get. I remember Daddy would always ride by Aultman's on the way home for lunch to see if they were busy, and also I'm sure so he could see whose car he saw in front of their store. I have a feeling Bobby Aultman did the same when he went home for lunch.

I remember spending the night with Gary Payne one Friday night and my feelings being hurt when I saw the groceries on the table. I realized that Mrs. Payne shopped at Aultman's instead of Goddard's. It was personal. I'm sure Stevie, my good friend and classmate, had the same experience when he spent the night with someone who had shopped at Goddard's Store. Stevie's dad owned Aultman's Store. We were competitors, but we were also friends.

One Friday afternoon on a holiday weekend my brother George was packing some chickens in ice to get ready for the busy weekend. We had about 12 boxes of chickens left, and we were wondering if we had enough to get through the weekend. Daddy walked up to George and told him to put six boxes aside for Aultman's Store. Daddy said that Bobby had just called and he was out of chickens so we were going to give him half of ours. George's response was that if we give Aultman's half our chickens, we will run out by Saturday morning and our customers will be upset. Daddy did not hesitate in his response. "There may be a time when we run out of chickens and Bobby will certainly return the favor." We did run out of chickens that weekend, and our customers did get upset, but I never forgot the lesson.

If the two local doctors did not completely spoil the citizens of Reynolds by making house calls whenever someone got sick, the Aultmans and the Goddards finished spoiling them. When I said that Reynolds had two full service grocery stores, I meant it.

The first way they were spoiled was that nobody had to pay for their groceries. It was not unusual to work all day and be very busy and not have any money at the end of the day. Customers charged their groceries. There were no credit cards. That means someone would push their buggy full of groceries up to the check-out counter, the cashier would add it up, and the customer would say, "Charge it, please." Sometimes the customers would pay up at the end of the month, and sometimes they would get behind.

Many customers would not even go to the trouble of coming to the store. They would order their groceries on the phone. We would then fill the order (which could be several pages) and deliver the groceries to the house. When we got to the house with the groceries, the lady would be sitting in a chair watching television and tell us to put the cold stuff in the refrigerator and the frozen stuff in the freezer. And they would tell us not to forget the bottles on the steps outside. When I say I have been in everybody's refrigerator in Reynolds, I mean it. Mrs. Louise Bryan lived less than a block away. She would call and order a six pack of diet cokes and tell you to bring them to her house and open one up for her when you got there. And so was life in Reynolds. But it was so good.

As I mentioned at the beginning, my family also ran the local funeral home. When I was really young, those two businesses were in the same building. Later the funeral home was moved across town. But our family spent most of our time working in the store because it was a daily job. We only worked at the funeral home when someone died. If fact, when someone died during the day, people knew to call the store to notify us. At night, they called the house, which had the same phone number as the funeral home.

Many of the young guys who grew up in Reynolds worked at Goddard's Store at some point in their life. They were exposed to the importance of having to work to earn money, but they were exposed to much more.

There were a couple of ladies who worked in that store for all of their adult life. Miss Ruth was the sweet one who was always encouraging. Mrs. Virginia was the slave driver. She was always in a hurry and always kept a pencil behind her ear. She could be as mean as the devil himself. These two ladies were opposites, but they complimented each other well. I learned later that there will always be Miss Ruth's and there will always be "Miss" Virginias in life. We need them both to make us better people. I think these two ladies working as a team had something to do with the future success of many people who worked at that store in their form-ative years.

My grandfather, who was better known as "Big Daddy," also contributed to the success of more than a few people, or maybe to their downfall. Big Daddy always spoke his mind and never trusted too many people. When I was growing up his office was in the back of the store. Every now and then he would come up front and sit in a chair so he could watch people to see if they were stealing. If he had even a remote idea they were stealing, he didn't mind accusing them of it, whether they were actually stealing or not.

Big Daddy must have liked Mrs. Virginia the best. Maybe it was because she worked there the longest. I think that he liked her better because I remember watching him hand out Christmas checks. He would write a check to Mrs. Virginia for $35 and write one to Miss Ruth for $25. And he would make sure they both saw what the other was getting. This practice extended to family members as well. I remember one Christmas Big Daddy called my brother George and me into his office to give us a Christmas gift. He wrote a check to me for $20 and wrote one to George for $10. Again, he made sure we both saw what the other got. I always figured he knew I would be the one to take over the family business and George would get as far from it as he could. In the end, his assessment would turn out to be correct.

I hope you are getting the picture of what it was like for a young lad to work at Goddard's store. We experienced a healthy mixture of "nice" (Miss Ruth), "mean" (Mrs. Virginia), and straightforwardness (Big Daddy). And there were others who worked there for many years.

My Daddy was the glue that held it all together. If it wasn't for him, the business would have folded. Mrs. Virginia would have run off all the help. Miss Ruth would have given everything away. And Big Daddy would have run off all the customers. Daddy was a businessman and people person and one of the most talented people I have ever known. He could do anything. If someone needed a small appliance repaired, they would bring it to him. If someone's TV went out, they would call Daddy. When someone's rifle was not shooting straight, they would ask him to fix it. If their fishing reel needing reworking, Daddy was their man. If their well quit pumping water in the middle of the night, they would call Daddy. If someone had a young boy or girl who needed encouraging, they would reach out to Daddy for help. If someone needed a letter of recommendation, Daddy would write the letter for them. If someone was sick, they would call Daddy to take them to the doctor. If someone died, Daddy would be the first person they called. I would venture to say that there are at least a few people who came from Reynolds who would give Daddy some credit for their own success in life. He was a role model, and he was a man's man. And he was my hero.

Daddy, whose real name was Edward McCoy

Goddard, was known by everyone affectionately as Ed. He could not stand for anyone to call him Mr. Ed. He always insisted that Mr. Ed was a horse. Some young people had a hard time calling him Ed, but he made them do it.

Hanson was a special man who worked at Goddard's Store for over 60 years. Hanson was Daddy's right-hand man. He did it all, from digging graves to digging wells. One Saturday night in the early 60's, a certified redneck who was obviously intoxicated came in the store and began to curse Hanson. Daddy was watching the situation closely, and I just knew something was about to happen. When the drunken man called Hanson the N-word, Daddy took matters into his own hands. He grabbed the man by his shirt collar and literally threw him out the front door of the store onto the sidewalk, warning him to never set foot in the door of that store again. Remember, this episode happened in the deep South in the early 1960's. It tells you something about the integrity of my dad. We never buried anyone in that man's family after that, but I can tell you, it was okay.

I think it important to tell you a little more about Daddy because you will find his footprints throughout the pages of this book. You will find his footprints to be big, too. He actually wore a size 16 shoe. He always told everyone that during the war he left his shoes on the beach and the Japanese bombed them, they thought they were PT boats.

Daddy was born in 1918 in Reynolds. He grew up to be much of a man. He was 6'3", and I just told you about his shoe size. When Daddy was a young man, someone stole a garden hoe from the store. Big Daddy sent Daddy to get it back. Daddy found the man who had stolen the hoe walking across the city park one day and walked up to him and hit him as hard as he could right between the eyes. The man was motionless on the ground and didn't move for a few minutes. Daddy lost his knuckle that day, but that particular thief never stole from the store again.

After he graduated from college, Daddy moved to south Florida where he met his future wife, Naia Gonzalez, who would later become our mother. They soon moved back to Reynolds, where he joined the family business. It was a real challenge for Naia to make the transition from Fort Myers, Florida, to Reynolds, Georgia. But she did, and Reynolds would become her home and she would play a vital role in the lives of many young people.

Daddy was very proud of his service in World War II and loved his country. He served in the Navy and was a lieutenant when the war ended. He always stood when the national anthem was played and stood at attention with his hand over his heart when the flag went by.

Daddy was also proud of his town. He was about as civic minded as a person could be. At his funeral, he was eulogized as being "Mr. Reynolds." Daddy loved Reynolds and was always working some angle to try to make it better.

Mama was the spiritual leader, not only for her children, but for most of the children in town. In her prime, she dedicated her life to serving young people through her church. She was a long-time Sunday school teacher, youth choir leader, Methodist Youth Fellowship leader, and she hauled kids all over the state from one church to another and from one camp to another. Most kids who grew up in Reynolds will give some credit to Naia Goddard for her spiritual influence in their life. In the latter years of her life, she dedicated her life to serving the elderly. In those years, she would make her rounds in her car and pick up the "old ladies" who could not drive anymore. She would take them to the store, the post office, the bank, and wherever else they wanted to go.

I never remember going to bed in our house when Mama didn't come in my bedroom, sit on my bed, and pray with me, and for me. I also remember the whole family gathering in my parent's bedroom many nights and reading the Bible together and praying together. And she insisted that we all pray. And we did.

Jessie Mae King

As were most southern towns in the early sixties, Reynolds was very segregated. Not only did the blacks and whites go to different schools and different churches, but they also went to different restrooms. I vividly remember seeing signs on restroom doors plainly stating "Whites Only." Crooks Restaurant, which was a typical southern family restaurant, changed its name to "Crooks Private Dining Club" when the desegregation laws came into existence. When you got to the front door, Mr. Crook would look to see who you were and he would hit a buzzer that would unlock the door to let you in. There were two waiting rooms at the hospital. The front room was for the whites. The blacks had to come through the alley to a back waiting room. The main wing of the hospital was for white patients. The back wing was for the black patients. The blacks lived in two different sections of town called "bottoms." The section across the railroad tracks was called the "Big Bottom." On the south side of town there was a settlement called "Goddard's Bottom." My great-grandfather owned that land at one time. Many of the white families had maids. It was not unusual to see a white housewife driving through town with her maid sitting in the back seat by herself on the way to work. The maids cooked, washed, cleaned, and kept the kids. When the family sat down to eat a meal, the maid would eat by herself after the family had finished, and many times they would drink out of a mason jar instead of using the regular glasses. Many younger readers will have a hard time believing all that, but trust me, it is the truth.

Now you need to understand, as bad as all that may seem, there was an upside for the black community. Many of these ladies were uneducated and untrained and had no way of making a living except for working as domestic workers in these homes. The black men who did not have a job would work in the "white folks," yards. They would usually be fed on a picnic table outside, and they would drink out of mason jars too.

We had a maid who worked at our house. Her name was Jessie Mae King. She waited on us hand and foot as long as I can remember. She cooked the best fried chicken and hoe-cake cornbread I have ever eaten, and her beef stew could cause a fight at the table.

Jessie lived in a literal shack in Goddard's Bottom. Her husband died at a young age, and Jessie was left to raise four children alone. They had no running water, and their bathroom was an outhouse located in the yard. Their only heat came from the wood they burned in their stove. Their house consisted of two rooms. One room is where they all slept, and the other room was a little kitchen. There were no monthly welfare checks in those days. Their only income was whatever Jessie earned working at our house. The clothes they wore were hand-me-downs that we gave them. Most of their meals came from leftovers at our house.

The interesting thing is that her children all became

very productive members of society. Her oldest son had a career in the military. The two girls moved to California and became very successful. Her youngest son, Billy, married and stayed in Reynolds to look after his mom.

Daddy was determined to help get Jessie and Billy out of that shack. In the early seventies his determination paid off. Jessie and Billy and his family moved into a brand new three-bedroom house, complete with running water, restrooms, and central heat and air. If anyone ever deserved a new house, it was Jessie Mae King.

Jessie was always a very important part of our family. She had full authority to discipline us and all the other kids that were in and out of our house. And she did. She would break a branch off a tree in the back yard, and make a switch, and she would wear us out with it when we disobeyed her. Sometimes her discipline would be misdirected.

Scott Posey spent about as much time at our house as he did his own. He and my brother George were a couple of years older than me and were always doing things to aggravate me. They told me one day that they had formed a club, and I could join it only if I went through the initiation. I had to jump out of the window naked and run around the house one time. I really wanted to be in the club, so I figured I could do that with no problem. So I took off all my clothes, jumped out the window, and ran around the house. When I got back to where I had jumped, they had closed the window. I had to go to the front door and ring the door bell, without a stitch of clothes. Jessie came to the door, and there I stood as naked as I came into the world. She wore my bare bottom out with a switch from a peach tree that day. I always thought that George and Scott should have been the ones getting the whooping. I never did join their club.

Every time there was thunder and lightning, Jessie would make us all sit still and be quiet. She would always say, "The Lord is talking – we better listen." Whenever we got sick, Jessie would be right there tending to us and making sure we got better. And she would always pray for us.

I always believed Jessie had a direct line to God. She had a child-like faith, and I kind of think God smiled on that. If any of us had a real need, we would always get Jessie to pray. She did not have much education, but she had more wisdom than any person I have ever known.

I never saw Jessie get angry. I never heard her say an unkind word about anyone. I never saw her lose her patience, and she was never rude. Jessie kept no record of wrongs and never tried to get her way. She found no delight in evil, but always rejoiced in the truth.

Jessie will never receive accolades from this world for what she accomplished in life. She does not have a place on her wall where she hangs her diplomas and certificates of achievement. She never had any money in the bank and never even drove an automobile.

The truth is she spent her life on earth serving our family.

I have a strong feeling our family will spend an eternity serving her in heaven.

As I write this, Jessie is 96 years old and is still alive. I drove over to Reynolds and picked her up and took her to our house to spend Christmas Eve a few months ago. I can tell you this: She did not eat leftovers and she did not eat after we got through eating. And she certainly did not drink out of a mason jar.

We brought out the fine china, and she sat at the head of the table. After the meal, we all sat at her feet and listened to her wisdom. And I was reminded of the words of Jesus in Matthew, "Blessed are the pure in heart, for they shall see God."

Today, the world is much different than it was in my little world during those years I grew up in Reynolds. Values have changed and priorities have changed. Life is much more complicated.

I believe most of us spin our wheels today worrying and dealing with things that don't make a hill-of-beans difference in the big scheme of things. Because we spend our energy worrying about what may happen tomorrow or what happened yesterday, we miss the moment. Life becomes so stressful that we miss the joy of living. We don't even enjoy the people we love the most. Our lives become miserable, and we make those around us miserable. And we take ourselves way too seriously.

Then, because we are miserable and we live with people we have made miserable, we start to look in the wrong places to get our needs met. We turn to things and/or people who will temporarily mask the pain and despair. And life becomes a vicious cycle of heartache. The result is we live our lives in a way God never intended us to live. And maybe we miss the important truths of life.

For me to tell you some of those important truths of life, I need to take you on a little trip. Please bear with me and stay with me until we get to the end of the trip. I really do have something to tell you. And if you stay with me, just maybe you'll never be the same.

From Evinrude Motors to Hoop Cheese

In 1866, (now that's not 1966 but 1866), my great-grandfather moved from Macon, Georgia, to Reynolds, Georgia, to start a business. He did that because he thought Reynolds was on the verge of becoming a "booming" city. I don't understand what my great-grandfather, E. A. Goddard, was thinking. There were only 1,200 people living in Reynolds in 1866.

Today, there are still only 1200 people living there!

After my great-grandfather had been in business for about 20 years, my grandfather came on the scene and worked with my great-grandfather. And then about 30 years after that, my dad came on the scene and worked with my grandfather. (My great-grandfather had died by then.) And then, about 30 years after that, I came on the scene and worked with my father and grandfather in this general store in Reynolds, Georgia. Their motto when I was growing up working in this family business was "We sell everything from Evinrude Motors to hoop cheese."

Trust me, they did.

When I was growing up working in that store, my dad was the Browning gun dealer; he was the Wilson Sporting Goods dealer; and he was the GE Appliance dealer. He sold the first television ever sold in the county and even went to school to learn how to work on them. He dug wells, he put the pumps in, he was the local insurance agent, and he sold groceries, meats,

Evinrude Motors, and hoop cheese!

I remember that when a lady would come in that store, she would get her grocery buggy, and her first stop would be the produce counter. That's pretty normal for a lady coming into a store that sells groceries, among everything else. Her next stop would be the frozen food counter. I'll never forget what happened there one day. I was a kid and I had no idea the "pictures" I was seeing would help form me later on in life.

I've got to tell you something about my Daddy. I don't know how else to say it, but my dad lived at the right time. He couldn't get by with this today, but Daddy used to love to hug and kiss all the ladies. Now, don't get nervous, he wasn't a pervert or anything like that. Everybody loved Daddy.

But there was a Methodist preacher who had recently moved into town and he was young and had a cute wife. Daddy was always hugging on her and calling her "sweetie" or "sugar." This particular day, this lady was bending over the frozen food counter, trying to pick out her frozen food. Daddy walked by in his normal fashion and sort of patted her on the rear end and said nonchalantly, "How you doing, sweetie?" The surprised lady almost turned the counter over when she wheeled around! She was a complete stranger. Daddy looked at her very calmly and said, "Excuse me lady. I thought you were the preacher's wife."

When you left the frozen food counter, the next stop would be the meat market. Now this was one of those old fashioned meat markets that you don't see anymore. Today, when you go in a store, they have the meats all wrapped, labeled, and priced. You pick out what you want out of the meat counter and go pay for it. But our meat market was one of those where you told the butcher what you wanted and he would go back in the back and cut it for you. If you wanted three pounds of hamburger meat, you would literally point out to him what you wanted him to grind. If you wanted three pork chops, you would get him to bring the loin out and you would tell him what part of the loin you wanted sliced.

I have this vivid memory of a lady standing at that meat counter one day holding a fryer (chicken) up to her nose. You have to picture this: she was holding one leg with one hand and the other leg with the other hand and was holding the chicken up to her nose. To be honest, it was quite a sight!

Daddy walked by and said, "Frances, what in the world are you doing?"

She answered defiantly, "Ed, I am trying to smell this chicken to be sure it is fresh."

Daddy kept walking, then hesitated and looked back with a funny look on his face and said, "Frances, do you think *you* could pass that test?"

At any rate, I was standing at that same meat market one day. Again, I was a young kid and I didn't realize the pictures I was seeing would help form me later on in life. But a lady was ordering her roast. She was telling the butcher exactly what she wanted. The butcher turned around to go back to cut the roast, and she stopped him. "I need to ask you something," she said. "Did anyone pass away last night? "Yes, in fact, Mrs. Jones died last night," the butcher replied. The customer said, "Then while you are cutting that roast,

I'm going to go to the back, sign the book and pay my last respects."

We had a funeral home behind the meat market.

And you talk about one-stop shopping!

Today, you can go in these super Wal-Marts and get your groceries, your clothes, your medicine, your furniture, your appliances and anything else that money can buy. We were doing that 100 years ago in Reynolds. Think about it. Wal-Mart doesn't have a funeral home in the back of it!

Now you have to admit that I've lived a pretty unique existence. You think about it, growing up in the Reynolds that I have described, being in all the businesses we were in, and also being in the business of burying people I've known and loved all my life. Listen, I know everybody in Reynolds. I've been in everybody's house. My goodness. I've been in everybody's refrigerator in Reynolds!

But it is very important for me that you know where I am coming from. I want you to know that I know that death is tough stuff. Just a few years ago I lost my Mama and Daddy only a few months apart. I can tell you, I got a new understanding of what I had been doing all my life. I've buried a lot of people's Mama and Daddy. But when I buried my own, I began to get a new understanding of what I had been doing.

But because of what I have done all my life, and what I still do in a different way today, I've made some observations about life. I call my observations *View from a Hearse*. I've been viewing life from a hearse since I was a little kid. Folks, I can't help it – that's just the way I see it.

Chapter Two

THE WORLD AIN'T GONNA STOP WHEN YOU DIE

"Whatever you are worried about today won't make a bit of difference to your loved ones when they visit your grave."

Don't Worry Guys, She Will Be Fine

The first observation I've made about life while viewing it from my hearse – and I hope you guys reading this don't get mad with me (I'll just say it anyway) – is "The world ain't gonna stop when you die!" I have thought about it many times as I drove a hearse in a funeral procession. As you ride through town leading the long line of cars, you see people going in and out of stores. Sometimes people pull over in their cars out of respect, but you look in your rearview mirror and you will see them take right back off after we get out of the way. I've seen the guys working on the side of the road take their hard hats off and hold them on their hearts as the funeral goes by, and in just a minute they put their hats back on and get right back to work. Life just keeps right on going.

Most guys get up in the morning and look at themselves in the mirror and think, "Man, I'm important! If something were to happen to me, my wife would be in a mess!"

I hate to tell you this, guys. But she will be fine.

I'll never forget the morning I was making funeral arrangements for a man who wasn't much older than me. I had known him and his wife all my life. She was understandably very upset. I was trying to get information for the newspaper. She was crying and I was crying. You have to trust me; there was nothing funny about anything we were doing. But we got to the part of discussing where her husband was going to be buried. She asked me to drive her out to the cemetery so she could show me where she wanted him buried. We drove out to this country-church cemetery. I almost had to drag her out to that lot when we got to the cemetery. She was distraught, and rightfully so. I was upset. But I learned something that day.

She stood at the foot of that family grave lot and pointed down and in a crying voice said, "Bruce, I want you to bury him right here." Of course, being the undertaker I am, and seeing the potential future dilemma, I put my arm around her and gently asked her if she was sure she wanted him buried in that particular space or if she wanted me to move over one grave space so there would be room for her when she died. I'll never forget her abrupt change of emotions and her staid response:

"No, I don't want to be buried here. I'm getting remarried!"

Now, there's nothing wrong with getting remarried. But I learned something that day: The world ain't gonna stop when you die!

I've Got to Feed the Chickens

I also remember our farmer friend who lost his wife after a lengthy illness. He was well liked in the community and was a very practical man. We had a gigantic church funeral and, as normal, finished the service at the committal in the cemetery. When the preacher said "Amen" and I knew the service was over, I walked under the tent and quietly spoke to the grieving widower. I told him there was a large crowd of people there who I'm sure wanted to speak to him. I asked him if he would like to stay seated and let the people file by or if he would rather stand up and mingle with the crowd. I'll never forget his response.

"No, I better go. I've got to feed the chickens!"

Now, I'm sure the chickens needed feeding. But I was reminded again that day that "the world ain't gonna stop when you die!"

Looking Forward to the Big Day

My memory bank is full of experiences and people who brought out the best in me and got the most out of life. One of those people was a lady named Miss Flootie. I called her Miss Flootie. Daddy called her Flootie.

Between my granddaddy, daddy, and me, we buried five of her husbands. She actually had a pretty good thing going. What she would do is she would find a man who had plenty of insurance and who was a little bit sick, and she would get married to him. We not only buried them when they died, but we helped her get the beneficiary changed before they died. Because of the beneficiary thing, Daddy was her hero.

I remember when one of her husbands died, I was home from college and Daddy was out of town. Rannie, our part-time employee (who also happened to be a preacher), and I went to a hospital in southern Georgia to make the removal. Miss Flootie didn't want me there. She wanted my dad, "Mr. Ed," and nobody but him. I tried to explain to her that I was Mr. Ed's son and that Mr. Ed would be at the funeral home when we got back to Reynolds. I thought I was going to have to show her my driver's license to prove who I was. Thank goodness Rannie was there. She recognized him because of his preaching and knew he worked for Daddy. I honestly believe if he hadn't been there with me, I would have had to come back without that body.

I also will never forget the next time I had to deal with her. It was a few months later and I had now graduated from college and was back home working at the store. Daddy and I were standing at the front of the store that day, and I heard Daddy say in his comical way, "Here comes Flootie – looks like she has a new husband with her!" He also said, "Bruce, if you are going to be in this business, it is time you learned to deal with her."

So, I took a deep breath and walked out in the parking lot. I was bothered by the fact that she was blowing her nose in her hand, but I held my hand out anyway. I greeted her with these words, "Miss Flootie, I don't know if you remember me, but I am Bruce, Mr. Ed's son."

She quickly replied and all in one breath said, "I remember you, Bruce. I met you at the hospital. And I want you to meet my new husband, and I want y'all to bury him too."

I shook his hand, and not knowing what else to say, I said, "It's great to meet you and we sure will be looking forward to it."

They came on in the store. She had his insurance policies, and we did all the necessary paperwork to make Miss Flootie the beneficiary. Everybody seemed really happy. I was thinking that they both seemed to be really looking forward to the big day.

Would You Get Remarried?

Lewis Grizzard used to tell this story, and I've told it many times myself. The husband and wife of many years were lying in bed. He was asleep. She couldn't sleep. She tapped him on the shoulder. Startled, he jumped up and asked her what was wrong. She said, "I've got something on my mind and I can't go to sleep!" "I hope it's important," he said. "You know I've got to go to work in the morning."

She replied, "It's very important! I wouldn't have awakened you if it weren't important. What I want to know is, if something happened to me and I passed away, would you get remarried?"

"Why in the world are you worried about that tonight? You ain't even sick. Can't we talk about this in the morning?"

"No, I want to know right now."

He replied, "No, I wouldn't. I would live by myself the rest of my life."

"That's all I wanted to know. Now I can go to sleep!" she replied.

He rolled over and went back to sleep. In a few minutes, she tapped him on the shoulder again. He jumped up and asked, "What in the world is wrong now?"

She said, "I've been thinking about what you just said. I believe I would want you to get remarried. I can't stand to think of you living by yourself the rest of your life!"

"Honey, I'll get remarried. Whatever you want me to do. Right now, all I want to do is to go to sleep. I've got to get up in the morning!" He rolled over and went back to sleep.

A few minutes later, she tapped on his shoulder again. Completely exasperated, he wheeled around and noticed she was sitting up in the bed. She said, "Honey, I'm really bothered by this conversation we are having."

"Honey, this is *your* conversation! All I'm trying to do is to go to sleep!"

She said, "I've been thinking about what you just said. If something happens to me, you're going to get this new woman. I've got to ask you something."

"Are you going to let her live in our house?"

"Honey, I reckon I will. The house is about paid for. It would be crazy for me to go out and buy another house, for goodness sakes. I'll probably let her live in the house. But please let's just go to sleep. I've got to go to work in the morning. He rolled over and fell asleep again.

A few more minutes went by and she tapped him on the shoulder again. He jumped up and she was standing up in the bed! She said, 'I can hardly get my breath; you've upset me so much! You said if something happens to me, you're going to get this new woman! And then you are going to let her live in *our* house! I've got to ask you another question."

"Are you going to let her wear my clothes?"

"Honey, you've got three closets full of clothes," he said. "Half of 'em you have never worn. It would be crazy for me to throw out all those good clothes! I'll probably let her wear your clothes."

She then went from sad to mad. She jumped out of the bed and started pacing the floor. She finally came over and got in his face and said very plainly, "Now let me be sure I understand what you've told me. If something happens to me, you're going to get this new woman, and you're going to let her live in our house, and you're going to let her wear my clothes! I've got to ask you one more question."

"What is it?" her husband reluctantly asked.

"Are you going to let her drive my sports car?"

"Absolutely not," he replied calmly.

"Why is that?" she asked.

"Because she can't drive a stick shift!"

I've Found another Match

My good friend Jim, who was in the monument business, told me this story. A lady had lost her husband and had come to his place to order a monument for her husband's grave in a small country-church cemetery. As she was placing the order, he explained to her it would take about four weeks for the monument to be installed. The monument would have the name, birth date, death, date, etc. inscribed on the front.

About two weeks later the lady came back and asked if she could have something inscribed on the back of the monument.

Of course, he told her that she could – it was a big monument and had plenty of room on the back – and that he charged "by the letter."

She asked him if he would have these words inscribed on the back of the monument: "The light of my life has gone out."

He said he could. He made the changes to the order, and a couple of weeks later the monument was installed in the cemetery.

A couple of weeks after that, the lady came back to Jim and told him the monument looked very good, but she was wondering if he could add something to what she had inscribed on the back of the monument.

Of course, Jim told her he could – it was a big monument and there was plenty of room, and they charged by the letter.

She said she wanted to add these words to what was already inscribed: "But I have found another match!"

The world ain't gonna stop when you die.

Do You Know How Many?

Karona (pronounced Karoni) Wainwright could have made a million dollars if he had an agent. He could have been the star of one of those funny sitcoms that we watched on television all the time in the seventies. If there ever was an outdoorsman, it was Karona. If there ever was a character, it was him. He wore his hair greased down and combed straight back, and he always had a little bit of a pot belly. He always had a funny story and always a joke to tell. You had to look around to be sure no women were standing around when Karona started one of his jokes.

His grandmother died, and the funeral was held at the chapel of the funeral home. Karona's mother and his aunt were obviously grieving about their mom's death, and Karona had done a good job consoling them and really taking care of them during the visitation and the funeral. He was very serious and concerned, and I was very impressed and proud of Karona. I had been successful in not getting in a conversation with him during those few days of the funeral process because I was afraid he might tell me a joke that was inappropriate at a funeral visitation or funeral. He was liable to tell such a joke at any moment.

We finished the funeral that day, and the family and friends got in their cars for the processional to the cemetery for the burial. I was driving the family car. I was by myself in the front seat, and Karona was in the back seat with his mother and his aunt, who were uncontrollably crying. In fact, he was seated between them and had his arms around both of them. I could see them in the rearview mirror.

Out of the blue, in the midst of the crying, Karona asked me a rather interesting question.

"Bruce, how many people does it take to eat a possum?"

I didn't know what to say. I didn't want to be rude so I answered. "I don't know. How many?"

"Three. Two to watch the traffic."

I didn't laugh, but I almost pulled the steering wheel out of the column to keep from it.

Karona reminded me again that the world just keeps on going after we die.

What Time Is It?

Although Daddy loved to have a good time and enjoyed joking around and having fun, he was a chronic worrier. He got to the point that he would be worried if he didn't have anything to worry about!

I was sitting by him in church one Sunday at the Reynolds United Methodist Church. I noticed he was writing all kinds of numbers all over the bulletin. When we stood up to sing, he kept figuring. When we sat down, he figured some more. I was wondering what in the world he was figuring on, but I could tell he was worried about something. Maybe he had a note due the next day, or maybe he was trying to figure out what somebody owed him. Whatever he was doing, there was one thing I was certain about. He did not have a clue about what was going on in the church service. He hadn't heard a word anybody said.

Plainly printed in the church bulletin was the title of the sermon for the day, "What Time Is It?" Of course, everybody in attendance had seen the title of the sermon, except Daddy. Brother Johnson was the preacher and fortunately had a great sense of humor. When all the preliminaries were finally over, Brother Johnson stood in the pulpit and began his sermon with these words, "What time is it?"

All of a sudden, Daddy looked at his watch and instinctively blurted out for everyone to hear, "Twenty-five minutes till twelve!"

Brother Johnson was laughing so hard it took a few minutes for him to gain his composure to continue with the sermon. Daddy went right on figuring and worrying and probably never knew he disrupted the church service.

For some reason every time I go by the cemetery to visit my parents' graves, I remember that Sunday morning.

I always think whatever he was worried about that Sunday is not very important today. The world kept right on turning after his death. And I will just go ahead and tell you. Whatever you are worried about today won't make a bit of difference to your loved ones when they visit your grave.

Chapter Three

LIGHTEN UP!

" . . . a cheerful heart is good medicine."

Get off the Phone!

Somebody Might Be Dead

The second observation I've made about life, viewing it from a hearse, is that we need to *lighten up*! It really is okay to laugh. Did you know that the Bible says that a "cheerful heart is good medicine" (Proverbs 17:22). As I have spoken to various groups, I've noticed something that really bothers me. Some guys have to get permission from their wife to smile!

It really is okay to laugh. It's good for you. I believe there are people who are in their graves prematurely (if that can happen), and I believe there are people who are chronically ill because they have never seen the lighter side of life. I can tell you, if I couldn't see the lighter side of life with what I have dealt with most of my life, I would go nuts!

You won't believe what happened.

At the end of 1960, Daddy moved the funeral home from behind the meat market across town, and all of a sudden we had a new funeral home. He bought the Methodist parsonage and completely gutted it and remodeled it into a funeral home, with chapel and all. Although I was a little child, I was absolutely flabbergasted. I thought all funeral homes were in the back of a grocery store!

We lived a block from that funeral home. You have to understand, in a town the size of Reynolds, it was not like we kept a secretary at the funeral home from

9 to 5 every day. We didn't go over there until some-body died. Of course, that could sometimes be three months in Reynolds.

We had one black rotary-dial telephone in the hall of our house. It was on one of those little built-in shelves in the wall. That was back in the days when everybody had only one phone, and it was usually in the hall. We also had one black rotary-dial telephone on the desk at the funeral home that was a block away. And we had only one phone number. Of course, this was way before answering services and pagers and cell phones.

Everybody has cell phones these days. I hardly ever have a speaking engagement when someone's phone doesn't go off.

I was driving north of Atlanta one morning and had to go to the restroom. I saw what looked like a brand-new convenience store when I got off the I-75 exit, and I thought this would be the perfect place.

The truth is, I was in a hurry to go to the restroom. I hurried through the convenience store and into the men's room. I was not thinking and walked (or ran) up to the first stall, ripped the door open, and, to my surprise, someone was in the stall. I scared him to death and he scared me to death! I apologized and decided to skip a stall and go to the next stall.

That's a man's thing, ladies, in case you didn't know.

Anyway, I got to the third stall and it was dirty, so I had to go back to the second stall. By the time I got in the second stall, the man in the first stall said in a loud voice,

"How you doing?"

Of course, I wanted to be nice. I had already embarrassed the man to death, so I answered in a loud voice:

"I'm doing fine."

A few seconds went by and the man asked another question,

"What time did you leave this morning?"

I'm thinking and wondering who in the world am I talking to in this public restroom three hours from home. But again, I wanted to be nice, so I answered,

"I left about 6:30."

About that time, the man in the next stall said, "Let me call you back, every time I say something, the guy in the next stall is trying to answer me!"

The man was talking on his cell phone.

I can tell you I had to put my feet up in that stall until he left. No way was I going to meet him at the sink after all that.

But anyway, we had only one phone in the hall of our house and one phone at the funeral home, and Daddy trained his kids well. When the phone rang in the hall of our house, we would rush to it and answer it, "Goddard Funeral Home." If we simply said, "Hello," we would get slapped. Being in the funeral business, the telephone was our livelihood. The truth is we were in bondage to the telephone. We couldn't all go to town at the same time. The biggest fight I ever got in with my brother George was in deciding who was going to stay home and answer the phone when everybody else went to town.

Because of all that, I hate telephones today. You can ask my wife. Today when I get on the phone, I say what I have to say and get off. I just don't linger "shootin' the bull," talking on the phone. I remember when I was a kid; I would be at home, sitting on the floor in the hall, talking on that black rotary-dial telephone. Daddy would walk by and slap me on the back, "Get off the phone, Bruce! Somebody might be dead!" I would hang the phone up in a hurry. That's why I'm still paranoid when I talk on the phone. Somebody could be dead somewhere!

Low Sick

Daddy and Mama used to get in all kinds of predicaments getting somebody to answer the phone so they could get out of the house.

You have already read about Jessie Mae King. Sometimes Daddy would leave Jessie at the house to answer the phone. As I have mentioned, she had more wisdom than most anybody you would ever meet, but she did not have much education. But she was real good about coming over to answer the phone. I'll never forget one special night.

Mama and Daddy were invited to go next door to Dr. Whatley and Rosemary's house to eat supper. Remember, Dr. Ed Whatley was one of two doctors in town, and he and his wife lived next door to Mama and Daddy and were their lifelong friends. Daddy took Miss Jessie in the hall and said; "Now Jessie, if you don't mind, sit in this chair in the hall so you can hear the phone ring. It is very important that you answer it as soon as you can get to it. Somebody might pass away! Here is a pad and a pencil. You write down the name of who called and the phone number and come next door to Dr. Whatley's house and get me."

Sure enough, that night a call came in. I was a little kid, but I remember her taking the message. I also remember she did not write anything down. She hung up the phone and walked next door to Dr. Whatley's house. "Mr. Ed, somebody's done dead!" she exclaimed.

Daddy asked her, "Jessie, did you get the name of the person who died?"

"No, to tell you the truth, they never told me. But they were really upset!"

"Jessie," Daddy replied calmly, "did you get the phone number of who called?"

"No, to tell you the truth, when they got upset, I got upset."

"Jessie, you mean to tell me that somebody has passed away and the family has called our funeral home to come get the body, and you didn't get the name or the phone number of who it is?"

"Mister Ed, you and Dr. Whatley are sittin' right here. Don't y'all know somebody 'round here that's been low sick?"

Daddy and Dr. Whatley had to drive all over the county that night trying to figure out who died. Thankfully, Dr. Whatley pretty much knew who was on the "list," and they were able to figure it out.

Sounds Like Him There

Speaking of telephones, one practice that people don't do anymore has to do with long-distance calling. I remember when parents, in an effort to save money, used to make their kids who were going out of town call home "collect" and ask for themselves, so they could be sure their kids got where they were going safely. People don't do that anymore. The truth is I never understood it. My thinking is why didn't they just go ahead and spend the 10 cents and talk to their children.

But my Mama used to do it.

My brother Mac, who was 12 years older than me (he still is 12 years older than me), went to college at the University of Minnesota. He only came home about twice a year. On one of those trips, I went with Mama and Daddy to take him back to the airport in Atlanta for his trip back to Minnesota. The last words Mama told him when he walked through that gate to get on the airplane were, "Mac, when you get to Minnesota, the first thing you should do when you get there is to call home *collect* and ask for yourself, so I can be sure you got there safely."

The first problem in this little plan was that he got to Minnesota before we got home from the Atlanta airport.

The second problem was that Jessie was answering the phone that night.

You know how the operator used to do. "I have a collect call for Mac Goddard. Will you accept the charges?"

Jessie responded, "I'm sorry but he ain't here."

Mac realized that Jessie had answered the phone. "Operator, I'll call back later."

Jessie's response was quick and priceless. "Operator! That sounds like him there!"

Telephone Answering Device

I'll never forget when the first answering machines came out. They were really big and heavy. You needed six pallbearers to get it in the house! I think we got the first one to hit our town. Daddy was so proud of that machine. Finally, he had a little freedom. He didn't have to have someone like Miss Jessie to stay at the house to answer the phone. It was wonderful. I'll never forget the message he had on that machine: "Hello, this is Ed Goddard and *this* is a telephone answering device. I will be away from this phone for a short time; however, I can be reached promptly by calling the Reynolds Golf Course. That number is 847-4546."

I can't imagine having a message on the funeral home phone saying to call the golf course. But we did.

What made things worse, Chuck, the man who ran the golf course, was sometimes not the most cordial fellow you would ever meet. And I don't think he really enjoyed having to take death calls at the golf course. He would have to get in a golf cart and ride out on the golf course to find Daddy to tell him somebody had died. I remember one Thursday afternoon vividly. I was playing golf with Daddy and his buddies, Wade Lane and Dr. Whatley. We were on the number four green, lining up our putts when we saw Chuck driving up in the golf cart. I remember Wade's reaction. "Oh, no, here comes Chuck; somebody must have died. This golf game is about to be over."

Chuck pulled up and said rather disgustedly, "Ed, Mr. Strickland is on the phone and says he has an emergency and needs to talk to you." Of course, we were all thinking the same thing. Wade said it out loud, "Something must have happened to Mrs. Strickland."

I rode with Daddy in the golf cart back to the pro shop. When he went inside to talk to Mr. Strickland, I began taking my golf shoes off. I figured Daddy would need some help to go pick up Mrs. Strickland. In just a few seconds, he came storming out of the door shaking his head. I asked him if something had happened to Mrs. Strickland. "No," he said, "Mr. Strickland said he bought some bacon in the store last week and he was getting ready to cook some of it and he noticed today's date was on the package. He wanted to know if it would be okay if he ate it!" We had come all the way off the golf course for that call. I remember telling Daddy that he really needed to change the message on that answering machine.

We did change the message but continued to use the answering machine to give us some measure of freedom. Call forwarding and cell phones would come much later.

This photo was taken in the mid-60s inside
"Goddard's" Store. Notice the old fashioned meat market
and the weekly special banners.

The funeral home was moved to this home from the back of the
general store.

Jessica Mae King is surrounded by Bruce's family on Christmas Eve 2004. We used the fine china that night and Jessica sat at the head of the table. (L-R) David, John, Kathy, Luke.

Bruce and Kathy in 2005

Special guests were in the audience.
President and Mrs. Jimmy Carter enjoyed Bruce's presentation.
Both laughed throughout the event.

Ed and Naia Goddard, the best parents God ever created.

Four generations of Goddards. L-R, George, Bruce, Ed, and Mac.
Front row, "Big Daddy" and Mac's son, Michael.

The Reynolds Depot

Our life time neighbors, Dr. Whatley and Rosemary. He delivered Bruce and she helped raise him.

The original marquee still stands in front of Goddard Funeral Home. Notice the phone number only uses four numbers.

The Bruce Goddards are ready for a big 2004 Christmas. (L-R)
Luke, John, Kathy, Bruce, and David

The Goddard brothers--Mac, Bruce and George.

Mid 60's photo of the Goddard family. Front row L-R, Naia, Bruce, Ed, and George. Back row, Joe, Kikky, Annis, and Mac.

Life long friends that helped create wonderful memories--Billy Bell, Jimmy Childre, Marsha James, Chuck (Woochie) Byrd.

The Cost of Answering Machines

I took a call one night from a lady whose husband had just died in Atlanta. I recognized the name and knew they were originally from Butler, which is the county seat of our county and about ten minutes from Reynolds. Edwards Funeral Home was located in Butler. Since we had never buried anybody in this particular family, I was surprised that the call did not go to Sonny Edwards.

The widow came to Reynolds the next morning to make funeral arrangements. The process was very simple. She bought the most expensive funeral we offered and wrote a check for payment-in-full on the spot. She then told me that there was no reason to keep the funeral home open. She had said she would just meet us at the cemetery the next day.

I was thinking this was probably the easiest money I had ever made. Funerals can be very involved and complicated, and a lot goes on behind the scenes to cause everything to be carried out smoothly. Stress is part of that. But there was no stress involved with this funeral. As she was getting ready to leave, I was still wondering how we got the call.

I walked her to the door. We had said our good-byes. Then she turned to me and nonchalantly said, "You know, I called Edwards Funeral Home to handle this, but I got one of those answering machines, and I can't stand to talk on those things. So, I just called you!"

I knew it was a thousand wonders she didn't get an answering machine when she called me. I just happened to be at home when she called.

I later told my friend Sonny how much it cost him to use that answering machine. We both agreed he could have almost hired someone to answer the phone for a year for what that cost him. I just happened to be the lucky one that night. I've never asked him, but he probably got a call or two from people who got my answering machine.

But it was worth it to both of us to be able to get away from the phone every now and then.

Greg Who?

Some years later, I hired our family friend, Camille, to work as a part-time receptionist at the funeral home. By now, I was not only running the funeral homes, but I was speaking all the time, I was chairman of the county recreation commission, I was the county coroner and I also had a discount-furniture business. People who needed me found me by calling the funeral home.

Looking back, it had to be difficult for Camille to walk in one day to start a part-time job and begin answering the phone for me. The call could be for a pending death or a death that had already happened. The call could be for someone wanting me to speak at their banquet. Someone could be in need of the coroner, which could include everything from a car accident to a shooting. It could be from a customer who was waiting for the delivery of a sofa or even from a mother whose son's batting helmet did not fit. There was definitely a variety of calls that came in to our funeral home, and it would obviously take anyone a few days to get acclimated to such variety.

I was on the way to Mt. Olive cemetery one afternoon when Camille called me on my cell phone. This was when cell phones first came out and they only worked in a few places, so I pulled off to the side of the road when she called so I could hear what was being said. Camille began the conversation something like this: "Bruce, you just had a call from a 'Greg' who wanted you to know that he has a flat tire."

Puzzled, I responded, "Greg who? And where is he?"

Camille told me that Greg did not tell her where he was, but he sounded like I would know where he was and that he was expecting me to help.

"Camille, did you get his last name or a phone number?" I asked while wondering if I had lost my mind completely.

I could hear the sound of paper before she replied, "His last name is Dickencrew – Greg Dickencrew!" She spelled it out: "D-i-c-k-e-n-c-r-e-w. He did not leave a number, but I assumed you would know the number."

I was getting worried now. "Camille, I have never heard of a Greg Dickencrew." I was racking my brain by now, trying to think if I knew someone by the name of Greg Dickencrew. I was worried if my friend (who I had forgotten about) was somewhere on the side of the road with a flat tire and was waiting on me.

I asked again, "Did he say where he was?"

Camille was getting confused now. "Bruce, he sounded like you would know exactly where he was and that he was expecting you to do something to help."

I told Camille again that I had never heard of a Greg Dickencrew and had no idea where to look for him. I told her if he happened to call back to let me know.

I continued on to the cemetery trying to remember if I went to school with a Greg Dickencrew, or if I had met him at a speaking engagement. I was concerned that someone was stranded on the side of the road.

As I pulled in the cemetery, to check on the grave for the funeral that day, I noticed the vault truck was parked close to the tent, and I was wondering why the truck was still there that close to the funeral hour.

As I got closer, my brain's light bulb began to flicker.

The vault truck had a flat tire!

I asked the grave crew if one of them had called the funeral home to tell me about the flat tire. Spam, the head gravedigger, told me he had called.

All of a sudden it hit me! It was not Greg Dickencrew! It was the "gravedigging crew!!"

Camille almost had it right.

Going Out in Style

I'm not sure when Braswell's Department Store opened up in Reynolds, but it was in operation in the seventies. I remember Miss Emiline Childre and Miss Blanche Powell working there. Most of their business came from shoe sales they would have once a month. There would be people lined up all the way down the sidewalk trying to get in to buy those shoes. I assume they were real cheap, although I don't ever remember buying shoes there.

What I do remember is going in that store after I was an adult and back home running the funeral home. An elderly lady had died, and I was preparing her body for burial and realized I was out of ladies' undergarments. Just as a reminder, when someone died in Reynolds, everyone in town would know it. If someone died at 3 a.m., I could go to the post office at 9 a.m. and everyone would want to know about what happened to whoever had died. It was just the way it was in Reynolds. When the light came on at the funeral home, word would get out quickly.

Anyway, I decided to go to Braswell's to pick up some ladies' undergarments for the funeral home. I walked in the store and Miss Emiline, who was my friend Jimmy's grandmother, greeted me as usual. I told her I needed some ladies' undergarments.

"I know exactly what she wears," was her immediate response.

I was thinking that it really didn't matter at this point, but if she knew what kind the lady liked, then I would sure get those. She went over to this counter and picked up some black, lacy, bikini underwear. Miss Emiline told me she had bought these before.

I was thinking that I cannot believe this 95 year-old-lady wore this kind of underwear, but I was assuming Miss Emiline knew something I did not know. Miss Emiline seemed to be excited that she had just what I needed, so I sure didn't want to say anything to the contrary.

When I was paying, Miss Emiline said something about how my wife also liked a certain kind of hose.

The light bulb began to come on at that point.

"Miss Emiline, who do you think these undergarments are for?"

"Well, I assumed they are for Kathy."

"Miss Emiline, these are for Miss Creekwater at the funeral home."

I laughed, and she laughed, and I was still laughing walking to my car. When I got to the car and looked back in the store, Miss Emiline was still laughing.

Miss Emiline and I were very close to sending this dear old lady out in style.

The Man Ain't Dead!

I'll never forget the first death call I went on. I was only 13 years old and Daddy decided that was the magic age. Truthfully, I cannot imagine carrying a 13-year-old with me on a death call. But Daddy could imagine it, and in his mind, I was just the right age. I look back on that night and realize now that my daddy started me at a very young age in this business. But somebody had died out in one of the suburbs of Reynolds, and all of a sudden, I found myself riding shotgun in the hearse.

I remember being very nervous that night. On the way out, I was worrying about whether I could even pick up my side of the stretcher. My goodness, I was just a little kid. I had hung out at the old funeral home at the store and at the new funeral home, and I knew how things worked, but I had never been on a real live death call. We drove way out in the country, and when we pulled up at that house I had never seen so many cars in my life. There were cars on both sides of the road and people everywhere. There were people standing in the yard. They were standing and sitting all over the front porch. People were going in and out of the front door. I couldn't believe it. I was already nervous but all this made me more nervous. I was thinking that the man who had passed away must be very important.

But I learned something that night.

I don't know how it is where you live, but where I

come from, there is something about death that makes people think of 'tater salad. You can be in the waiting room at the hospital. The doctor can come out of the operating room, pull the mask off his face, call the family together, and say, "I'm sorry, but grandpa didn't make it." And many times you will hear these words, "Oh, my Lord, let me go home and make some 'tater salad!" I don't know what it is about 'tater salad that helps people through the grieving process, but somehow it does.

That night I began to realize that maybe this person was not that important. Maybe everybody was just bringing 'tater salad to the house. For some reason, that knowledge made me feel better that night.

Daddy left me standing by the hearse as he went in the house. I suppose he went in to find out exactly where the person was before we came in the house with the stretcher. Finally, he came back, and I helped him take the stretcher up this big flight of steps I had been worriedly eyeing on the front of the house. We were suddenly on the front porch with the stretcher. People were getting out of the way as they usually do when an undertaker is rolling a stretcher close to them. All of a sudden, Daddy surprised me and told me to roll the stretcher through the door and into a room. He said he would be back in a minute, but he wanted to go talk to the family. Remember now, I was only 13 years of age.

I rolled the stretcher in what I remember as a very large room. I saw the man lying on the bed. I rolled the stretcher next to the bed. Those stretchers under-takers take with them do adjust. I knew how to do that, having hung around the funeral home all my life. I started to let the stretcher down so it would be even with the bed. About that time, I thought I saw the man move! I backed up. I was thinking surely this man is dead. They wouldn't have the funeral home out here with all this 'tater salad if the man wasn't dead.

After a moment I got my composure and eased back up to the bed. I'm thinking I'm really too young to be doing this. I was sure I was hallucinating. I was also saying out loud, "Daddy, please hurry up!" About that time, I looked down at the man on the bed, and he reached up and scratched his nose!

Again, I wasn't but 13-years-old. But you don't have to be a rocket scientist to understand. They are outside picking out pallbearers, and this man is lying in the bed scratching his nose: we've got problems!

I started to go outside to find Daddy. I met him coming in. "Daddy, I need to talk to you," I said quietly. Daddy replied, "Bruce, we can talk in a minute. The family is ready for us to move him to the funeral home."

"Daddy, I believe I need to talk to you before we move him to the funeral home."

Daddy looked at me with a funny expression. I whispered in his ear, "Daddy, the man ain't dead!"

Daddy looked at the man lying on the bed and then pointed in the other direction. To my astonishment, I realized that the man who was dead was on the other side of the room sitting in a chair! The man I had been dealing with was the dead man's invalid father.

It's a wonder I stayed in this business after that night.

But there is a moral to this story. When the undertaker comes to your house, be doggoned sure they get the right fellow.

He's In A Nursing Home

About the time I got out of school and was starting my career, Daddy and my brother Mac, decided to purchase Bankston Funeral Home in Roberta. Roberta is located about 14 miles from Reynolds and is similar in size.

Billy Bankston had a long-time friend, Henry McAfee, who had assisted him in the funeral home for many years. Henry knew everybody in Crawford County and knew where everybody lived. He owned a general store in town and was very well thought of all over the county. Being from another county and the fact that we were somewhat strangers in Crawford County, we desperately needed Henry to stay on and work with us at the funeral home. We were very glad when Henry agreed to stay on. Henry never charged us for helping us, nor would he accept any money. He always said, "Just bury me when I die, and we will be even!" Henry loved to laugh and had a unique ability to see the lighter side in life. I think that is why he and my dad got along so well.

Not long after we took over the funeral home in Roberta, we received a call in the middle of the night about a death in Crawford County. It was not our first death call at our newly acquired funeral home, but it was one of the first. Mac called Henry to meet us at the funeral home so he could show us where to go and introduce us to the family.

Mac drove the hearse, Henry was in the middle, and I was in the passenger seat as we drove in the driveway of this house in rural Crawford County. As usual, there were many cars in the yard, and it was obvious that a large number of family and friends had gathered at the home.

There was one young man standing in the driveway. Henry immediately recognized him as Tommy, the son of the deceased. Tommy stopped us as we drove in and gave us explicit directions as to where to back the hearse. He stood in the headlights and directed us as we backed up to the steps in the back of the house.

When we got out of the hearse, Mac and Henry went on in the house to talk to the widow. Tommy opened the back door of the hearse before I got a chance to get around to the back. I introduced myself to Tommy, expressed my sympathy to him, and explained to him I appreciated his help, but he did not have to assist us. He paid no attention to my comments. I also told him we needed to wait until Henry and Mac got back, and then we would go in the house with the stretcher.

Tommy insisted we get the stretcher out and go on in the house. He was leading the way with one end of the stretcher, and I was following with the other end as we went up the steps.

As we went in the door, I realized we were in the kitchen and there was a crowd of people gathered there. People were looking at us with very weird expressions on their faces. I knew we shouldn't be in the kitchen with the stretcher, but I was kind of helpless at this point.

In an attempt to get the stretcher out of the kitchen, I motioned to Tommy to keep walking to the hall area. I asked him quietly which room his Daddy was in. I almost fainted when he responded loudly, "Oh, he's in a nursing home in Macon."

I wondered if he thought we carried a stretcher with us everywhere we went. I had to explain to Mac and Henry that the dead man was not there. I cannot explain the embarrassment as we went back out of the house with the empty stretcher. I can still see the people standing in the yard looking at us and wondering what in the world we were doing. I'm sure everybody there was wondering what kind of crazy people they had running the funeral home in Roberta.

When we later told Daddy about this strange experience, he laughed and said we should be very grateful that Henry was with us. If he had not been there, we probably would have never gotten another death call in Crawford County.

One Way to Wet Your Pants

Many years later I had another experience that I will always remember. I was running the funeral business. A gentleman whom I did not know had died at a relative's residence while he and his family were visiting in Taylor County. When I arrived at the residence to make the removal, I went in the house to talk to the family. I talked to a very upset widow for a few minutes and then set an appointment for her to come to the funeral home the next morning to make arrangements to have her husband transported back to their hometown. As I stood up, one of the family members stood up with me and quietly told me the deceased was lying on the bed in the bedroom down the hall.

I walked down the hall and stood at the doorway of the bedroom. I could see the gentleman lying face down on a large bed on the opposite side from where I was standing. I could tell we were going to have problems getting in the bedroom with the stretcher because there was not enough room to make the turn in the hall. There was also a table that had to be moved. I went outside and told my assistant, B. R., of the situation. We rolled the stretcher in the hall and moved a table and a lamp. I stepped into the bedroom and had figured that I needed to slide the deceased toward the side of the bed where I was standing.

When I reached across the bed to grab his legs to begin the process of sliding him to my side of the bed, to my absolute shock and horror, the man jumped up!

I knocked a lamp off a table getting out of the way. B. R. let out a cuss word that I know could have been heard by the neighbors. Truthfully, we both almost wet our pants!

We quickly realized we were in the wrong room. The deceased was in a bedroom down the hall. We were in another bedroom. The deceased's son was lying on the bed trying to deal with his grief.

I cannot imagine what he must have thought. I think we scared him as much as he scared us.

Fast-Thinking Undertaker

One of the questions I get asked, especially by ladies, more than any other question is this:

"Do you split a man's coat in the back before you put him in the casket?"

The real answer to that is pretty simple, actually. The answer is you do if the coat doesn't fit.

When I was in mortuary school, we had a teacher who was a retired funeral director from Oklahoma. He told us he used to split all the coats. He also said he lied about it. When families would ask him if he split the coat, he would always say no. He figured they wouldn't understand it, and it would serve no purpose to try to explain it to them. He said he felt bad about lying, but he never told the truth about splitting coats until one day when a lady came in the funeral home to view her husband who had passed away. Before going back to the viewing room she asked the funeral director the question, "Did you split my husband's coat?"

Of course, he gave her his usual answer. "No, I certainly did not!"

"Well, thank goodness," she said, "because I gave you the wrong coat. The coat I gave you was my son's coat."

That undertaker didn't miss a beat. "Ma'am, I didn't split your husband's coat, but I'll have to split it to get it off!"

Now that is a fast-thinking undertaker. I like a fast-thinking undertaker.

Everything in the Grave Looks Fine

My grandfather, who we called "Big Daddy," was a stickler for carrying out funerals in the right way. He was concerned about every little detail, and this passion definitely was obvious to everyone who knew him and was passed down to my dad and me. I remember one incident when I was a teenager and was assisting on a funeral. Big Daddy was using a cane by then for walking, but he also used it for other reasons. On this particular day, I was standing outside the church before a funeral with my hands in my pockets. Big Daddy walked up to me and popped me on the leg with his cane and sternly said, "Boy, get your hands out of your pockets." I can tell you from that day on I never put my hands in a pocket during a funeral, nor have I allowed anyone who worked for me to do so. Big Daddy wanted everything to be carried out in a professional manner, and he did not mind telling me that putting my hands in my pockets was very unprofessional.

Mt. Olive Cemetery, which is located outside of Reynolds, is nothing but sand. It sits on the top of a hill and reminds me of a "boot hill" or a cemetery you would see in an old Western movie. Because of the sand, nothing can grow – like trees or grass. It is obviously rather desolate looking, and the sand also makes it very difficult to dig graves. Actually the digging is not difficult. The challenge arises because the graves have a tendency to cave in. As a funeral director, you constantly have to watch mourners to be sure they do not walk too close to the grave. Not only would we have to re-dig the grave, but a mourner could sink completely out of sight if not careful.

Big Daddy always seemed to enjoy reminding mourners of the danger of getting too close to the grave. He watched them carefully.

On one summer afternoon at a very large funeral, Big Daddy had been working diligently keeping people away from the grave. The service finally started and Big Daddy was standing in a dignified manner at the foot of the casket. Of course, he had his hands crossed in front, left over right, in the usual undertaker's stance. All of a sudden, right in front of God and everybody, the grave started to cave in, and Big Daddy slowly sank into the grave. With the stunned crowd watching, the surprised preacher stopped speaking and walked over and grabbed Big Daddy's hand and helped pull him out of the grave.

With the preacher's help, Big Daddy got back up, stood back in the undertaker's stance, and announced calmly to the shocked mourners, "Everything in the grave looks fine."

Now that is a fast-thinking undertaker.

Which Team Did She Play On?

A young man was working hard in one of the big chain grocery stores. He was running the produce department. This arrogant acting customer was looking at the lettuce and was grumbling about how much lettuce costs. He turned to the young man and said, "Son, I am not going to give you $1.20 for one head of lettuce. This price is absolutely ridiculous. What I want you to do is to take this head of lettuce, slice it in half, and I will give you 60 cents for half of it.

"Sir," the boy replied politely, "I can't sell you a half of head of lettuce for half price. You have to buy the whole head of lettuce."

"Son, you either sell me the half head of lettuce for half price or I'm going to take my business somewhere else. And I don't think the manager of this store wants to lose my business."

The young man, not knowing exactly what to do, walked to the back of the store and found the manager. "Sir, there is this jerk out here that wants to buy a half head of lettuce at half price." When he said that, the young man did not realize the customer was standing right behind him. The boy saw him out of the corner of his eye and quickly turned and said, "But this gentleman right here would like to buy the other half."

Now, he was thinking as fast as that undertaker I just told you about.

The store manager watched that customer pay for

his groceries and leave the store. He then called the young produce worker over to him and said, "Son, I have to tell you. I was very impressed with the way you just handled that situation. That man is one of my best customers. You got out of that situation as gracefully as anyone I've ever seen. Son, you could go a long way with this company." Then he asked him, "Where are you from anyway?"

The young man replied, "Chicago."

"Chicago?" He asked. "How did you get all the way to Georgia from Chicago?"

"Sir, I hate Chicago. Nobody lives up there but prostitutes and hockey players."

"Now hold on just a minute," the manager said. "My wife came from Chicago."

The young man quickly responded, "Really, which team did she play on?"

The Buzzards Will Carry Him Off!

Obviously, a funeral home is normally a very somber place. But I've got to tell you, some of the funniest things in the world can happen in the most somber places.

Not long after I came home to begin my funeral-service career, we received a call one morning about a fatality in a motor vehicle accident on the Fort Valley highway. We were told the deceased was from Alabama. The authorities in Fort Valley had contacted the widow and asked us to take the body to our funeral home, and the widow would contact us as to which funeral home in Alabama would be handling the arrangements.

Daddy talked to this lady, and she gave him the name of a funeral home she wished to use in Alabama. We then talked to that funeral home, and they asked us to embalm the body, and they would make arrangements to transport him to their funeral home, which was located near Montgomery. All of these details were made before Rannie and I left the funeral home in Reynolds to make the removal. Daddy was actually at our other location in Roberta, making these arrangements over the telephone. He called me and gave me this information.

We drove to Fort Valley to make the removal. On the way back to Reynolds, Daddy paged me. (Obviously, these were days before cell phones.) I knew it must be something important for him to be paging me knowing I was in the middle of the removal, so I pulled into a little store and called him.

He told me to leave the body at the hospital. He said he had just received a call from another lady saying she was the widow. In other words, we had two different ladies claiming they were married to this man. He told me to leave the body at the hospital until we could find out which one of these ladies was the real widow.

I explained to him that we had already picked the body up and that we were halfway back to Reynolds. I told him it would be easier just to take him on to the funeral home and figure out what to do from there. Daddy reluctantly agreed.

A problem I thought would be easily resolved turned into an all day and late night dilemma. Both ladies said they had been married to him for years. Neither of them knew about the other wife. One of the wives wanted him taken to a funeral home near Birmingham to be cremated. The other wanted us to take him to a funeral home in Montgomery. Obviously, we did not embalm him, not knowing who the legal person was to give us permission to do so.

This talking back and forth on the phone to the grieving (and astonished) widows went on all day. My brother Mac, who was in business with my dad, had also now come to the funeral home to try to figure out what to do. Everybody was there.

The widow from Montgomery finally drove to the funeral home that night. The parents of the deceased were with her. The parents told us this lady was the "real" widow and they didn't know about the lady from Birmingham. Of course, they wanted us to disregard the other widow, and we were trying to explain to them the legal ramifications for us and that we would be exposing ourselves to major liability if we did so.

My sister, Kikky, and her husband, Joe, happened to stop by Reynolds that night on the way to their home in South Georgia. Mama told Joe, who was a lawyer, that we had an unusual situation going on at the funeral home. He and my brother George drove over to check on us.

When Joe stuck his head in the doorway, Daddy was in the middle of explaining the legal challenges we faced releasing this body to them. He never broke his train of thought and suddenly announced, "Our attorney has now arrived, and he has come to advise us on this situation."

Of course, Joe had no idea what was going on. But he took the cue from Daddy and acted as if he had been called in to resolve this issue. It was beginning to resemble a circus.

You have to understand that this family was being treated with the utmost respect, dignity, and sensitivity. This was a very difficult issue for the family, and we all felt so sorry for the situation they were in.

A legal discussion was now going on between my brother-in-law and the family. They were discussing their legal options.

All of a sudden one of our assistants stuck his head in the door of the office and loudly stated, "I can tell y'all one thing! If y'all don't do something with him, the buzzards will carry him off!"

Daddy and Mac almost fainted. Joe didn't know what to say. I can just imagine the mental pictures that were developing for the family.

I do know one thing. After that statement, Daddy decided to risk some legal exposure and told me to start the embalming process.

Whatever the Family Wants

I have learned that people have all kinds of ideas as to what is important when their loved one dies. For instance, some people want a full traditional funeral, some would rather have only a graveside service, and some prefer cremation. Some people want the casket closed at the funeral home for visitation, and some would rather have it opened. Some are looking for the most expensive casket, some want the least expensive casket, and some want something in between. In other words, people have different needs and desires. Our job in funeral service is to do our very best to meet the needs of the family beyond their expectations. In my opinion, there is not a standard list of things that must be done to meet those needs because they vary so much from family to family. A phrase you hear often in funeral home circles is "whatever the family wants."

Normal requests from some families might be considered a little unusual to other families. I believe that's what makes America great.

A man from another town visited me one day at the funeral home to talk about his funeral arrangements. He had been recently diagnosed with cancer, and he knew the prognosis was not good. He told me he had a request that was a little unusual, but he was afraid his dog would not be taken care of when he died, and he wanted his dog buried with him. Of course, I was nodding and agreeing with whatever he wanted. I was just trying to appease an elderly man who probably didn't have long to live. Funeral directors are used to getting all kinds of requests from people that are usually never mentioned when their time comes.

As he was leaving, he asked me to come out to his car to meet his dog. Of course, I agreed to meet his dog. When he opened the door, I reached in the car to shake the dog's paw or pet him on the head. Undertakers shake hands with and pat everybody. The dog growled at me and snapped. I almost knocked myself out when I hit my head on the car door getting away from the dog. I was thinking that the man must have told the dog about his plans, and the dog was not very happy.

Several months later I received a call that this gentleman had passed away and had requested our services. On the way to make the removal, I remembered the conversation I had earlier with the man, but I did not think anybody knew it but him and me.

When we arrived at the house, we noticed that some of the mourners were taking turns holding a little dog. I realized this was the dog I had met earlier, and I was sure hoping the dog didn't recognize me.

We were going through our normal routine when the son asked to speak to me in another room. He asked if his dad had talked to me earlier about his funeral arrangements. Of course, I told him we did have a previous conversation about his funeral wishes. Then the son asked me if his dad had talked to me about burying his dog. I had to say that he did. I told him we could discuss the matter about the dog later.

The next thing I knew, somebody was attempting to hand a very angry dog to me. I told them that I would be glad to bury their dog but I had no way of killing their dog. I was wondering if they thought I would take the dog back to the funeral home and hit him on the head with a brick or something. I told them they would have to have the dog put to sleep if they wanted me to bury him.

As we were driving away, I was thinking surely they were not going to have that dog put to sleep. The son had told me that they knew that is what his dad wanted. I felt for the family because I knew they were just trying to carry out his wishes. I remember Jeff, who worked for me and was with me that night, saying, "They should ask the dog."

The next day when the family came in to make arrangements, I had decided not to mention anything about the dog. My hope was that they had decided not to have the dog put to sleep. We got to the end of the arrangements conference, and they told me that the dog was being put to sleep and they would bring the dog to me in a couple of hours.

I then told them I had nowhere to keep a dead dog for two days until the funeral. They spoke among themselves and somebody in the family offered their freezer to keep the dog in until the funeral.

The morning of the funeral, a man brought me the frozen dog wrapped in a towel.

Whatever the family wants.

Maybe This Was Some

Expensive Dog or Something

An elderly lady whom I had known all my life passed away. I made funeral arrangements with her children, who lived in the Atlanta area. After the arrangements conference, the children hung around town to give me time to get their mother ready for viewing. They wanted to view their mother before leaving to go back to Atlanta. They planned on returning to Reynolds the next day for the visitation and the funeral.

As is our custom and at the family's request, we had the casket open that afternoon for people in the community to come by, sign the book, and view the body. They usually come in one at a time or two at a time.

Late that afternoon, I noticed a late-model Mercedes drive up in the driveway. In Reynolds, a Mercedes will cause someone to take a double look, so the car got my attention. I noticed two very well-dressed young couples getting out of the car. I did not recognize them, but could tell they had a little more sophistication than we are accustomed to in Reynolds.

I greeted them when they came in the front door. I noticed that a dog came in with them. I was trying to meet their sophistication standards and introduced myself in a very business-like manner. They introduced themselves as grandchildren of the deceased. No one mentioned the dog.

I walked them and the dog to the back to the viewing room and closed the door to give them some privacy as they were viewing their grandmother. I thought it was a little unusual to bring a dog with you to a view your grandmother at the funeral home, but I wasn't about to say anything. I figured they were much more sophisticated than me, and maybe this was some expensive dog or something.

I went to my office and had been there about ten minutes when one of the young ladies came in and asked, "Is there anyway you can get that dog out of there?"

I had to do some serious apologizing to these sophisticated people.

I almost was bitten trying to drag the dog out of the building. I found out later that the dog belonged to our new neighbors, Butch and Beverly. They had moved in next door a couple of weeks earlier, and I had not yet had the pleasure of meeting Nubby, their beloved dog.

Can you imagine what those two couples were thinking when they were trying to view their grand-mother? I can just hear them standing in there saying, "What kind of crazy funeral home is this?"

Jimmy Swaggert Music

This incident happened during one of those weeks when we were extremely busy. We only had one funeral crew, so when we got busy with multiple funerals we could get really stretched out.

We had a graveside funeral scheduled at Mt. Olive for a lady who had been delivered to us from an out-of-state funeral home. In other words, they had already had a funeral in North Carolina conducted by a North Carolina funeral home, but the family wanted another visitation at our funeral home in Reynolds and then a service at the graveside.

I was surprised at how many people came to the visitation, which was held at the funeral home a couple of hours before the funeral hour. Our normal procedure for graveside funerals was to take the deceased to the cemetery about thirty minutes early. We would then bring the family in a procession to get to the cemetery at the funeral hour. The plan this day was that I would stay at the funeral home with the family and lead the procession. My staff would take the flowers and the deceased to the cemetery and get everything set up.

I helped my staff load the casket in the hearse and load the flowers. As they were about to leave, a family member came up to me with a cassette tape and asked if I could play the tape at the funeral. I told them I had no way to play the tape at the cemetery. The family member told me that he had a cassette player that I could use. Jeff, my main employee who would be in charge at the cemetery, was driving off in the hearse so I had to stop him. We waited on the family member to get the tape player. Of course, Jeff was highly concerned about how he would play a cassette tape at a graveside service – and rightfully so. I asked the family member how he wanted us to do it.

He explained that he wanted the cassette player off in the distance and wanted the music playing as background music as the preacher was speaking. I thought I could talk them out of that, but I told Jeff to take the tape and the tape player with him. I asked him to set it up on a monument off in the distance and to watch me when I got there, and I would nod to him when it was time to start the music. Jeff and I were both aware that when I got there with the family, the funeral would start, and we would not have an opportunity to discuss any of this when I got to the cemetery.

The family member was adamant that he wanted me to play the music as background music as the preacher was talking, and I could not change his mind. I could not imagine how that would work, but I wanted to please him.

When I drove up to the cemetery with the family, I noticed there was a rather large crowd of friends and well-wishers standing very solemnly at the graveside tent. I then saw Jeff standing, dignified, off in the distance behind a monument with the cassette player sitting on the monument in front of him.

I started to get tickled, but I knew I could not laugh. I just knew this was about to be a fiasco. When I got the family seated at the graveside, I looked out at Jeff and nodded to him. He looked at me as if he was saying, "Are you sure you want me to do this?" I nodded again.

He started the music that I now discovered was a tape of Jimmy Swaggert singing.

As soon as the music started, all the friends and well-wishers turned in unison to look at Jeff. They were taken by surprise at the sudden music, and they were looking at Jeff as if they were saying, "What in the world are you doing playing country music and disrupting this funeral?"

The preacher started talking. The crowd was alternately looking at the preacher and then looking at Jeff.

It was the funniest thing I have ever witnessed in my life. It was like two different things were going on. The preacher was trying to talk in time to this music that was playing off in the distance. It didn't work at all.

I was about to bust a gut. I could not look at Jeff, and he could not look at me. It was the most unusual ten minutes I think I ever spent at a funeral.

We got through with that funeral and left immediately for the next funeral. I never had an opportunity to even speak to Jeff about the whole debacle.

That night I exhaustedly climbed in my bed. I started laughing uncontrollably. Kathy thought I was losing my mind. I called Jeff on the phone. He answered and realized it was me, and he started laughing. I don't think we ever said a word to each other. All we did was laugh out loud for several minutes.

We had been holding that in all day and I can tell you – it sure felt good to get it out.

Second Opinion

As I have already said, some of the funniest things happen in the middle of things that are not supposed to be funny. I guess the fact that everybody is so serious is what makes it funny.

Daddy used to tell a very funny story about a death call he made one night. Two sisters lived together, and they were obviously very close. When Daddy got to the house that night to make the removal, Dr. Sams was there with the family. In those days, the doctor made house calls and almost always waited at the residence until the funeral director got there. The family always called the doctor. He would go out and pronounce the person dead, and then the doctor would call the funeral home.

This night was a routine death call. When Daddy arrived at the residence, he talked to Dr. Sams for a few minutes, and then Dr. Sams excused himself to continue on his house calls. Daddy, of course, visited with the family and set a time for the family to come to the funeral home the next day to make funeral arrangements. Daddy and his helper carefully placed the deceased lady on the stretcher and then in the hearse. As they were driving out of the driveway, the sister of the deceased ran to catch the hearse and knocked on the window. Obviously startled, Daddy got out of the hearse to see what the lady wanted. He discovered that she had a very unusual request.

She said, "Ed, I want you to know I love Dr. Sams. He is a wonderful doctor and has been wonderful to our family. I know he is a fine doctor, and I really appreciate him being here with us tonight. But I would feel better if you would let Dr. Whatley see my sister to be sure she is dead before you take her to the funeral home."

In other words, she wanted a second opinion.

Of course, Daddy told her that he would certainly honor her request.

It was about 3:00 a.m. by now and Daddy drove back into town and drove the hearse straight to Dr. Whatley's house. He got out and walked up to the front door and knocked.

Now, you need to understand, this was really not that unusual. Most funeral homes also operated the ambulance service and so did we. It was not unusual for Daddy to drive the hearse in the middle of the night to the doctor's house with a sick person to be checked.

So, Dr. Whatley wasn't very surprised when he opened the door and saw Daddy standing there.

Daddy was the first to speak: "Ed, I've got someone out here you need to check."

Dr. Whatley said, "Give me a minute and let me get my pants on. and I'll be right out!" In just a moment, Dr. Whatley came hurrying out of the house. He had his stethoscope around his neck and his little black bag in his hand. He opened the side door of the hearse and jumped in to check the little lady.

Daddy just stood back with his arms crossed and watched the whole situation unfold.

In just a few moments, Dr. Whatley stuck his head

out the door and exclaimed, "Ed, this lady is dead!"

Daddy didn't break a smile. "That's all I wanted to know."

What Did You Do With the Body?

I learned early on in my funeral-service career never to schedule a funeral until the deceased is physically at the funeral home. There are times when a family requests your funeral home when the death occurs in another town or state. In some of those cases, there are a few logistical items that must be taken care of before the deceased arrives at your funeral home, such as, necessary paperwork and airline reservations. Sometimes a family wants to go ahead and schedule the funeral so the family and friends can make plans. Sometimes this is done assuming that everything that is supposed to take place will take place as scheduled. Sometimes it doesn't work like that.

I remember on one such occasion, Daddy scheduled a funeral over the telephone for a family whose loved one had died in Florida. They were having a visitation in Florida, and the family would drive up the next morning for an early afternoon graveside funeral. The deceased was scheduled to fly into Macon, about 40 miles away at 9 a.m. Obviously, this would have given us plenty of time for an afternoon funeral. However, Daddy had broken our cardinal rule about scheduling funerals.

Rannie and I drove to Macon in the hearse and got to the airport in plenty of time for the scheduled flight. Our first discovery at the airport was the plane was going to be an hour late. That made us both a little nervous, but we knew we still had plenty of time. We checked with the attendant, and he confirmed that the body was indeed on the plane. When the plane arrived, we watched out the window as the crew unloaded the freight. As you have probably already figured out, the body was not on the plane. The attendant got in touch with the Orlando airport, and they discovered the body had been inadvertently left off the plane. The next scheduled flight was in about an hour. The problem was that the flight was not to Macon, but to Atlanta. We decided we could drive to Atlanta and get there by the time the plane did. To make a long story short, we picked up the body in Atlanta and "flew" in the hearse back to the funeral home. We made it at the last minute, but everybody was sweating.

I said all that to tell you about a similar experience that happened many years before I began my career. Big Daddy had scheduled a graveside funeral for a family friend who had passed away in another state. The body was scheduled to come in to Reynolds on the train the day before the funeral. For some reason, it was not on the scheduled train. They found out a mistake had been made at the train station, but the depot manager assured them the body would be on the train the next day. They knew that the time of arrival of the train would be very close to the funeral hour, but for some reason they decided not to change the plans for the funeral.

Big Daddy was at the cemetery with the family and friends, and Daddy was at the train station waiting on the deceased. Of course, the train was late. The body finally arrived, and it was loaded in the hearse. Daddy rushed out to the cemetery knowing that Big Daddy would be standing on his head.

Big Daddy was blaming the situation on Daddy when he arrived and was whispering rather loudly, "Where in the world have you been, Ed? What in the world have you been doing? You are thirty minutes late for this funeral!" Of course, there was not a thing Daddy could have done to get there earlier, but he bit his lip and never said a word.

The pallbearers took the casket out of the hearse and set it on the lowering device over the grave. The family decided they would have a last viewing, since they did not have an opportunity to have a viewing at the funeral home as they had originally planned. Still embarrassed and fuming because the funeral was starting late, Big Daddy proceeded to open the lid of the casket for the viewing. Of course, all the family and friends in attendance were watching as he opened the head panel in his sensitive and dignified manner.

Unbeknownst to Big Daddy, the little lady had slid to the foot of the casket during the trip. You can imagine his shock when he opened the casket and did not see a body.

All of a sudden, Big Daddy whirled around and shouted in a loud voice for everyone to hear, "Son, what did you do with the body?"

I can just imagine the collective gasp from the mourners.

Be Sure She Is Not in There

I mentioned Miss Flootie earlier and the fact that she was the beneficiary on the life insurance of five different husbands. But I need to tell you about the first time I ever came in contact with her.

I was around 14 years old and was helping Daddy on a funeral being held in the chapel at the funeral home. This wild-eyed lady came storming in the front door, talking in a loud voice saying she wanted to see Mr. Ed.

Of course Daddy (Mr. Ed) heard her when she came in the door and was first trying to quiet her down so she would not completely disrupt the funeral. He kind of held on to her arm and walked her into the first door he could get to, which happened to be the selection room – full of caskets.

I was okay with what was going on because I knew Daddy could handle any situation or anybody. I thought that until I noticed that this wild-eyed lady had a pistol in her hand. That scared me, so I followed Daddy and Miss Flootie into the casket room. I had no idea how to stop a potential shooting, but I was curious enough to go in behind them.

Miss Flootie was very upset to say the least. She was upset because she was convinced that Daddy was about to bury someone in her personal grave space. Today, the term for such an occurrence is what is known as a wrongful burial. Some lawyers and the clients they represent have made a lot of money the last few years representing families who sue cemeteries for wrongful burials.

But this happened long before we became such a litigious society, looking to sue our friends and neighbors for everything that ever goes wrong.

I will say that Miss Flootie had no desire to sue anyone. I actually first thought she was there to shoot the man who she thought had made such a mistake. But I quickly found out differently.

She was threatening to go out to the cemetery and shoot herself and be in the grave when the procession got there! She gave new meaning to someone wanting their personal space. I never met anyone who was willing to die for a certain place to be buried.

I was amazed at how well Daddy handled the situation. He explained to Miss Flootie that the burial was not in her grave space, and he had personally marked the grave and her space was actually on the other side of the grave where the burial was taking place today. I always wondered if he really knew that or if he was just hoping it was so to get the woman brandishing a pistol out of the funeral home.

Daddy drove the hearse that day in the procession to the cemetery, and I rode with him. I asked him on the way to the cemetery if he really thought that lady would shoot herself so she could be buried in the place where she wanted to be buried.

Daddy was completely at ease when he responded to me that Miss Flootie was just a little on the crazy side and was trying to get attention and would never, ever do something like that.

Those words sure made me feel better.

It was pretty quiet in the hearse the rest of the way to the cemetery. We finally pulled up at the cemetery with the long line of cars behind us and Daddy looked over at me very sternly and said, "Bruce, walk real calmly up to the grave and look in there to be sure she is not in there."

Jingle Bells

I've learned several things in my career as a funeral director. One of those things is that anything and everything can happen at a funeral.

I heard a story about a preacher from Macon, Georgia, who went to a little country church outside of a little town in South Georgia to preach a funeral for an elderly lady. It was very hot, in the middle of July, and he knew the little church would never hold the crowd that would be at this funeral. When he arrived at the funeral home the day of the funeral, the funeral director told him of an unusual request from the family.

According to the funeral director, the family had originally requested "Amazing Grace" to be sung at the funeral. A young man who was a member of the church had agreed to sing it. But the family had now changed their mind. They wanted her favorite song, "Jingle Bells," to be sung instead of "Amazing Grace." The funeral director wanted to know if the preacher had a problem with that.

The preacher's response was "whatever the family wants." However, he did request that the song be sung at the beginning of the service so he and the congregation could regroup.

The funeral director called the young man who had agreed to sing and told him of the change. The young man and the pianist rushed around at the last minute to find the music for "Jingle Bells," and he practiced singing this song in a dignified way that would be acceptable at a funeral.

The funeral hour arrived. The crowd was even larger than expected. All the pews were full, people were standing along the walls, and there were almost as many people standing outside as were inside. The loudspeaker they had rigged outside of the building would help. People were sweating. The hand fans were fanning. The advertising dollars were at work.

At the appropriate time, the young man stood and started singing in a dignified way, "Dashing through the snow..."

The people couldn't believe what they were hearing. Some were staring at the floor. Some just shook their heads. Some felt sorry for the young boy as he continued to sing,

"In a one-horse open sleigh – hey...."

The young singer was ready to find a hole to get in. The more he sang, the worse it got. Finally he finished the song.

After the committal service, the funeral director came up to the young man with a funny look on his face and made an unbelievable comment: "We've made a terrible mistake," he said. "The song they wanted you to sing was 'Golden Bells'." When they ring those golden bells!

Oh, my goodness. The young man had sung "Jingle Bells" at this poor lady's funeral. The preacher learned later that the family was sitting around discussing the requested song and decided to change the song to "Golden Bells." The son-in-law was anointed as the person to tell the undertaker.

The problem was, he didn't know "Golden Bells" from "Jingle Bells." He said he heard "Golden Bells" but he thought they were talking about "Jingle Bells."

The young singer never sang in church again. Last time anybody heard of him, he was working in a bar in Albuquerque.

The Funeral Is Being Held Now

Brother Hubert is a bi-vocational preacher from Potterville whom I have known all my life. For those that do not know, Potterville is a suburb of Reynolds. Brother Hubert was very active in the community when I was growing up. He coached little league baseball for many years and was a very positive influence on many kids in our community. He was a great encourager to us kids and has always been a very easygoing man. All the kids loved Brother Hubert.

He was also well respected by the adults. I know that because there is no telling how many funeral services he has preached over the years. He worked at Flint Electric most of his life, and most every time he preached a funeral, he would have to take off from work to do it. I wondered why he did what he did. Obviously, he knew people in the community very well and had close relationships with most of the people for whom he was called on to preach a funeral. But he was also willing to help us out when we got in a pinch for somebody he did not know very well. For those of you that don't know it, it is not the easiest thing in the world to preach a funeral for somebody you don't know very well. I've had to do it on occasions when the preacher did not show up.

I remember one such funeral. I gave Brother Hubert a clergy card at the last minute, which is in itself a dangerous thing. There is a lot of information on the clergy card, and it helps for the preacher to have a little bit of time to at least go over the card before he gets in the pulpit. Sometimes the funeral home can make an error on the card, and sometimes the preacher can make an error trying to read something to a live audience from a card he has never even seen. But I figured he would appreciate some information that would at least be some fill time for him during the service.

I was a little nervous when Brother Hubert started to read the clergy card that day to the audience. He pronounced the name correctly and was doing pretty good until he got to the death date. Where we were supposed to put the death date on the card, we had put the birth date and vice versa. He, of course, read the birth date for the death date.

His wife, Barbara, was playing the piano and caught the mistake. She got his attention and interrupted him by whispering rather loudly, "That is when she died, Hubert, not when she was born!"

You could tell Brother Hubert was frustrated. He continued to read the card. He stated when she was born, where she was born, when she died, where she died, the organizations in which she was a member, and named all the survivors. He got down to the line that stated when and where the funeral would be held.

"The funeral," he said as he looked up at the audience, "is being held now."

The funeral home staff almost went under the pews. It was like people were looking around and saying, "Is *that* what we are doing here??"

We have put Brother Hubert in some difficult circumstances over the years, and he has always obliged. But it's a wonder he did not kill us after that funeral.

His Name Is Not Smith!

Preachers were put on earth for several reasons. I am convinced one of the reasons is for the sake of an undertaker's levity. They can really do some funny things.

I'll never forget the graveside funeral we had for a man who had died in North Georgia. The deceased's wife had roots in Reynolds, but the deceased himself had no blood connections. The wife's family had not lived in Reynolds for many years, and because of that, they were not very well known. The family requested that I contact the Methodist minister in Reynolds to ask him to preach the funeral.

I called my friend, Steve, who happened to be the Methodist preacher at that time and told him of the situation. He agreed to preach the funeral and said he would come over to the funeral home to meet the family to get some information about this man he had never even heard of nor met. That evening, Brother Steve came over and spent almost an hour with the family. He asked a lot of questions, and I could tell the family was very impressed with the preacher and the effort he was making to make their service a meaningful experience for them.

The next day, I was surprised at how many people were at the funeral. It was very cold and windy. There were only a few people from Reynolds in attendance, but a pretty large crowd of people from out of town had gathered. We had two graveside tents set up and side curtains to break the force of the cold wind. The family was seated in the chairs and shivering under the tent, and the others were surrounding them.

The preacher began the service and mentioned that the service was for "Mr. Smith." He then began sharing life experiences of the "Smith" family. There was one major problem.

There wasn't a "Smith" in the crowd. The funeral was for Mr. Thomas.

As the preacher continued to talk, one of the family members got up from his chair and walked over to me and said, "You've got to do *something*."

I agreed and walked behind the side curtain. The preacher was just on the other side of the side curtain but could not see me. I listened for a few moments and was hoping he had just had a mental lapse and would get it right. All of a sudden, I heard "Smith" about three times in a row. I then walked to the other side of the side curtain and tapped on the preacher's shoulder. Obviously shocked, he stopped speaking. I then whispered in his ear, "His name is Thomas."

The totally stunned preacher didn't say a word for at least 30 seconds. His first words to the family after I absolutely blew him away were, "I am so sorry. I thought his name was "Smith." How he kept his composure to finish that service is beyond me.

Can you imagine going to your dad's funeral and the preacher never calling him by the right name? I would think you would have to go back and do it again.

That Was a Little Tight

On one service, I had picked the family up at their residence. I was driving the family car and leading the procession to the church for the funeral. As we were driving into the churchyard, one of the family members handed me a cassette tape and asked me to play it during the funeral service. My first question was "Is there a tape player in the church?" The next obvious question was "Where is it?"

When we pulled up at the church, which was right at the funeral hour, I asked the family to stay seated in the car. I got out of the car and explained to Jeff, who was working the funeral with me, the request the family had made. His response was something to the effect that surely I wasn't going to try to play a tape on a machine that I didn't know how to work in front of a church full of people without the benefit of testing it.

I told the preacher about the request. He just sighed and shook his head. I told him I would play the tape at the beginning of the service and then he would take over.

Jeff walked down the aisle to start the funeral and had the congregation stand. I walked in with the family behind the preacher. When I seated the family, I walked up in the pulpit area to play the tape. The tape player happened to be directly in front of the family.

The preacher, who happened to be a very large

man, was seated in the pulpit chair in the pulpit opposite from me.

My first challenge was I could not see the tape-
player controls. I had just walked into a relatively dark
room from the bright of the day. I was almost seeing
spots. Somehow I got the tape in and hit what I thought
was the play button. I hit rewind instead. I then fast-
forwarded it about as much as I thought I had re-
wound it. I then hit the play button and the song came
on very loud in the middle of the song. I looked up and
could see that Jeff and our helpers were getting tickled.
I was getting tickled as well but I could not think about
laughing. I was sitting directly in front of the family. It
ain't cool for a funeral director to laugh at a funeral. I
did not dare look at Jeff, who was standing in the back.
I got the volume adjusted and held my breath until the
song ended and I stopped the tape.

About that time I heard a noise that sounded like
someone dragging a piano across the stage. I looked
up and to my amazement, the preacher, who was
attempting to walk up to the podium, was stuck in the
pulpit chair. Or to say it better, the chair was stuck to
him. (When one's butt is wider than the space between
the armrests on a chair, this will happen.)

I got up from my chair and walked across the pulpit
to where the preacher was stuck and (in a dignified
way), pulled the chair off him.

The preacher then proceeded to walk to the
podium. I will never forget the way he began that
funeral service: "That was a little tight!"

The pallbearers were laughing. Jeff and our helpers
went out the door. I don't know how the family was

reacting. I couldn't look at them. I was bent over tying my shoes over and over. I was wearing loafers. Being that tickled in a place that is as serious as a funeral could cause one to have a heart attack.

The next day, I walked into a local restaurant for lunch. I spotted one of the pallbearers from the previous day sitting at a middle table. He motioned for me to come over to the table. I'll never forget what he said. And I quote:

"The preacher got his ass stuck in the chair yesterday, didn't he?"

I can beat around the bush with that all I want. The truth is that is exactly what happened.

Wives Can Do Anything

There was a period of time after Daddy had heart surgery that I had to coerce Kathy into assisting me with funerals. She was reluctant to do that at first, but the truth is she turned into a very good funeral person. I knew she would be good with people, but she surprised me how quickly she learned the business. But her learning did not come without a few interesting moments.

The first funeral she worked was a very big test. I would be bringing the family to the church in the procession, and Kathy would be working the church. I knew this was a very large family, and this was a very small church. I told Kathy ahead of time that we would never get everybody in the church. I told her to reserve most of the church for the family, and the others could stand along the walls or they could stand outside.

It turned out the number of family members who had gathered at the house and who would be coming with me in the procession was even larger than I expected. We would not even get close to getting all the family members in the church, much less the friends and well-wishers.

I arrived at the church with the very large family right at the funeral hour. Kathy was down front seating the family as they walked in the church. I was outside trying to organize that crowd because I knew there would be a large number who would not get in the church.

I was surprised at how many people kept walking into the church. I was wondering where in the world Kathy was seating them. I knew there was no way all these people could get in that church. I was totally flabbergasted that so many were getting in that very small church.

All of a sudden I looked around the side of the building, and people were coming out the back door! Kathy had filled up the seats and was directing the people through a back door which she assumed led to another room in the back of the church.

She was sending them out the back door.

They were circling back around the building and about to get back in line to go back into the church. Kathy would have been there forever seating that crowd if I didn't come to her rescue.

This was also one of those funerals when the family requested me to open the casket after the funeral and allow everyone to file by one last time to pay their last respects. This was a common occurrence years ago in rural Georgia, but it is not done very often anymore. Kathy was certainly not used to this, and I should have warned her before the funeral.

The procedure was exactly the same every time. I would walk down the aisle with my assistant after the benediction and then announce to the congregation that the family had made this request to open the casket a final time. I would then open the casket and direct the mourners, row by row, as they filed by the open casket and then returned to their seats. I would stand at the head of the casket and my assistant would stand at the foot as the people filed by. We did this for two reasons: One, we wanted to keep the line moving so we would not be there all day, and, two, we needed to be close because some people tended to want to get in the casket with the deceased. I guess that would be okay, but my concern was they would knock the casket off the stand it was sitting on if they leaned in too close. And then we would have a royal mess.

The other piece to this is that this was usually a very emotional time for the mourners. The crying would start small with the first row or two, but it would get worse and worse as people filed by. The fact is it would get very loud. Crying would quickly turn into wailing. The challenge was that most of the mourners would cry not because they were upset about the deceased but because they would get upset watching others cry.

Kathy fell right into this trap.

I happened to glance at her during the "last walk by," and Kathy was weeping. I had to walk over to console my assistant now along with all the other mourners. How do you tell your wife not to cry? I thought I was going to have to get her a navel orange.

One of the defense mechanisms some of the younger mourners were using that day was the navel-orange technique. I've seen that done more that a few times. Someone would cut a whole in the end of a large navel orange and suck the end of the orange. They would then pass the orange down the row and many would suck from the same orange. I never understood the significance of the orange except I figured they used it to keep occupied to keep from letting all their emotions out.

When that funeral finally was over, Kathy was an emotional wreck. I had to sit down that night and tell her she would end up in an insane asylum if she got that emotionally involved with every funeral. I told her I had thoughts that day that I was going to have to borrow the orange that was being passed around to let her take a suck to get her emotions under control.

If you get nothing else out of this book, maybe what you just read about will be worth the effort. The next time you feel the need to cry, get yourself a navel orange, cut a hole in the end of it, and start sucking.

When Kathy later went through menopause and her hormones started "backing up," I always kept a few navel oranges around the house. It works pretty well.

The Pallbearer Flowers

Kathy did learn to get her emotions under control (at least for funerals) after that and got much better at seating folks. She was learning quickly and was getting very good. But there was one more incident that I will never forget.

Our normal procedure at every funeral was to pin boutonnières on each pallbearer. We did this so the pallbearers could feel special and everyone would recognize that they were pallbearers. The boutonnieres we used were of the fake variety. They were made out of paper, but they actually looked pretty good from far off. We always had a box of these fake flowers at each funeral, and someone on the staff would be assigned the task of pinning the flowers on the pallbearers.

The funeral on this particular day was at a small country church. Kathy was charged with "running the church" while I was bringing the family to the church in a procession from their house. The church was packed that day. You could count on one hand how many of the male mourners would be wearing a coat and tie for funerals at this particular church.

I drove up with the family at the funeral hour and walked them to the door of the church to get them organized before going in. At my nod, Kathy would walk down to the front of the church and have the congregation stand. I would then escort the family into the church and seat them row by row. I would then walk back to the front of the church, join Kathy, and then I would direct the congregation to be seated. Kathy and I would then walk out of the church together, and the funeral would begin.

Everything was going perfectly. Kathy walked down and had the congregation stand in a very dignified manner. I was so impressed with the way she was handling herself. I brought the family down and seated them row by row. Everything was perfect. I walked back to the front of the church to stand with Kathy and was about to have everyone seated.

I looked out at the congregation and could not believe what I saw.

Every male in the congregation had a pallbearer flower pinned on them! Have you ever seen a boutonnière pinned on someone who is not wearing a coat? How about a church full of people with boutonnières pinned directly on their shirts?

I take full blame for this whole incident. I had told Kathy to be sure to take the box of flowers and pin them on. I think I missed the pallbearer part. She pinned one on everybody.

I can tell you I almost lost it in front of God and everybody that day. As I've said before, it ain't cool for the undertaker to be laughing during a funeral. I was definitely not cool that day.

Sometimes Things Just Happen

During my dad's later years, he got to where he did not hear very well. He called me down to their house one morning and told me that he and Mama had been hearing a rooster every morning, and they believed the rooster was under their house.

I walked outside and found the opening to the crawl space under the house. I got down on my hands and knees with a flashlight and looked the best I could under the house for a rooster. I saw no sign of a rooster.

I asked Mama and Daddy if they were certain they had heard a rooster. They were convinced there was a rooster under the house and not very convinced of the effort I made to find the rooster.

The next morning they called me to say they both heard the rooster again. I took a small man with me on this trip because I was too big to crawl under the house, and I really didn't want to do that anyway. Daddy and I stood in the yard at the crawl-space door while Pee Wee crawled all under the house looking for the rooster. Pee Wee found no sign of a rooster either, but I paid him for his effort and trouble.

Daddy was still certain there was a rooster under the house and was baffled why nobody could find it.

The next morning they called me again and said they heard the rooster again. I was thinking on the way to the house that they hear this rooster every

morning at the same time. I had a thought. When I got
to their house I picked up Daddy's watch. He had
bought his little cheap watch through a mail-order
house somewhere. I found the alarm on the watch and
played it. Sure enough, the alarm sound was the sound
of a rooster doing the cock-a-doodle-do! They had
been hearing the alarm on this watch every morning!

I told you all that so you can better understand this
story. Like I have said, a funeral is not the place for an
undertaker to be laughing. But sometimes the undertaker can cause others to laugh unbeknownst to the
undertaker.

This particular funeral was being held at our chapel
in the funeral home in Reynolds. Daddy was somewhat retired by now but still enjoyed working funerals,
and he, in fact, helped with most of them. He was at
the age that he had experienced some trouble with
some of his normal body functions, but his hearing
was such that it never bothered him in the least. If he
happened to hear a strange sound, he figured it was
someone else making the sound.

Again, I was with the family and Daddy was
"running the church." Among other things, that meant
Daddy was walking back and forth down the aisle
seating people as they arrived for the funeral. Please
understand – everybody at that funeral knew Daddy,
and he knew everybody there. Reynolds really was like
one big family. Everyone also knew Daddy would have
never done what he was doing in a million years if he
had known it was happening.

But it became apparent to the people in the congregation that Daddy was passing gas (noise variety) as

he was escorting people down the aisle. It was like there was a "putt putt" with almost every step.

You have to understand, the person who had passed away was like family to everybody at that funeral. They had come to pay their respects to their friend, and it was not a laughing matter. But Daddy's antics were about to crack everybody up. The fact that everyone knew that Daddy did not realize what was happening made it even funnier. As I have mentioned, I don't know what it is, but when you find yourself in a place where you aren't supposed to laugh and something really funny happens, it can cause heart problems trying to hold it all in. It's a wonder that there weren't a few heart attacks that day.

I knew nothing of this because I was with the family when all this was going on. After that funeral and before the committal service began at the cemetery, my nephew, Michael, came up to me and whispered to me what had happened during the funeral at the chapel. He was still cracking up. After the funeral, people kept coming up to me and telling me the same story – with tears in their eyes from laughing.

I decided I better speak to Daddy about what had happened, but I knew it would not be an easy thing to do because I knew he didn't know he was doing it.

Mama and Daddy came out the house that night, and I decided to bite the bullet and deal with the situation.

"Daddy," I respectfully said, "I don't think you realize it, but you were passing gas today at the funeral."

"I did no such thing!" Daddy replied adamantly.

"Daddy, you did. Several people came up to me and

told me you were passing gas as you walked up and down the aisle." (I was trying my best to handle this the right way.)

"Who said that? If someone said that, they are a liar! I would never do such a thing!" (Now he was really angry.)

I'll never forget Mama jumping in the conversation to rescue her son when she politely said, "Ed, now sometimes you do that, and you don't know you are doing it. In fact, you do that a lot."

I guess it pays sometimes to be hard of hearing. I'm also glad Mama had sinus problems.

The Emergency Hearse

As I said earlier, during my growing up years, it was common for small-town funeral homes to also be the ambulance service. We had to be on call for death calls, but we had to be ready at a moment's notice for an automobile accident or a heart attack as well.

I look back on those days with many questions. I guess what I am saying is this. I wouldn't want to be in the middle of a heart attack and have my undertaker come to the house to take me to the hospital in his hearse. But that is the way we did it.

I remember as a kid the excitement of going to an automobile accident in the hearse with the red light and siren flashing. My friends at school thought I had it made.

None of us had any training. We had an oxygen tank in the hearse, but I don't think there was even a band-aid in there. We just loaded them and hauled them. Not much science involved at all.

I remember riding in the back of the hearse one day with a man who had recently had surgery. He was at home, but they called us because he was in a lot of pain. Daddy was driving and told me my job was to sit in the jump seat next to the man on the stretcher and keep him company.

I could tell the man was in a lot of pain, but we had a pretty good conversation going. I was talking to the man and looking right at him when all of a sudden, he took a gasp of air and slumped over. I shook him, but it did no good.

I went up to the sliding glass window to tell Daddy what had happened. I told him that I thought the man was dead. Daddy turned on the red light and siren and in a few minutes pulled into Montgomery Hospital in Butler. A nurse came out and checked the patient. A few minutes later, Dr. Montgomery drove up and verified that the man was indeed dead.

I couldn't believe it. But I never forgot that day. I decided that day that I wanted to get some kind of training to be able to help people in the back of the hearse.

I had another similar experience, but this time a lady was in labor. She had gone to Sams-Whatley hospital in Reynolds to have her baby, and something went wrong. Dr. Whatley called Daddy to have her rushed to the Macon hospital.

Again, Daddy put me in the back; however, this time I wasn't having a conversation with a man. This time I had a screaming woman who I thought was about to have a baby any second. I wasn't even sure where babies came from at that point in my life. I was sure of one thing. I didn't want to be in the back of the hearse with this lady.

I again knocked on the sliding glass window. I told Daddy that I knew I was not old enough to drive, but I wasn't old enough to deliver a baby either. I told him I thought I needed to swap with him. "Let me drive, and you get back here with her!" I figured I could drive better than I could deliver a baby.

Daddy pulled over to the side of the road. He got in

the back with the pregnant woman, and I got up front and drove the hearse, with red lights flashing and siren screaming, to Macon. I was 14 years old.

I remember thinking again that I wanted to learn how to help people in the back of the hearse.

140/60

In the early 1970's, the laws in Georgia changed, and counties had to get in the ambulance business. In most communities, the funeral directors were the only ones with any experience in ambulance work, so it was logical that many funeral directors took the necessary training required to become EMT's. My brother Mac was the first to get the training in Reynolds. Daddy and Mac could not get trained at the same time because somebody had to be in Reynolds to look after the funeral business. I was in college at the time. When Mac got through with the training, it was Daddy's turn to go. Daddy talked his friend and neighbor, Julian Whatley, into taking the training with him. I decided to join them. I knew the class would spill over into my fall quarter at the University of Georgia, but I was ready to learn what I had wanted to learn since I was a kid.

We had an absolute blast in that class. I've never laughed any harder in my life than I did during that EMT class with Daddy and Julian. I learned a lot about what to do to help people in emergency situations. But I also learned that it really is hard to teach an old dog new tricks.

Early on in the course we had to learn to take each other's blood pressure. Julian and I passed our test with flying colors. We could tell Daddy was having a little trouble with his test. He had the blood pressure cuff wrapped correctly on the arm. He was holding the

16

stethoscope in the correct place on the fold of the arm to hear the sound. But I could tell he was having a hard time hearing the pulse. The nurse who was testing him started laughing. Julian and I saw what was happening, and we started laughing. Other students in the class caught on, and they started laughing. Daddy finally wrote his answer on the sheet: 140/60.

By then everyone was laughing hysterically.

Daddy had the earpieces of the stethoscope around his neck instead of in his ears. He just made up a blood pressure and wrote it down.

Somehow we all passed that class, but it was a wonder. But that fun class was the foundation for some of the funniest things I would ever experience as I began my career as an undertaker/ EMT.

A New Kind of Alcohol?

Russell Montgomery and I later went on to get advanced training sponsored by a nearby medical center. Our EMT friend from Butler, Ed Robinson, went with us. This was much more than just basic EMT work. They were teaching us about giving drugs and all kinds of things. This course lasted about a year, and it was very involved.

Russell was a farmer who lived in the Crowell community. He, his wife Barbara, and their son, Russ all became EMT's and worked part-time with the local ambulance service. All three of them later went on to become very good at what they did and ended up as paramedics and made a career out it.

When I got through with that class, I was convinced I had just enough training to be dangerous.

Part of the training included working at that medical center. We worked through different rotations, including a rotation in the emergency room, a rotation in the cardiac care unit, and, if I remember correctly, a rotation in labor and delivery.

One night while working in the emergency room, they had us assisting the nurses. The emergency room was very busy that night, and they needed all the help they could get. Someone with a medical problem would come into the emergency room. A triage nurse would determine if there was a real medical emergency. She or he would prioritize the cases and eventually send them in to see one of the doctors.

Russell's and my job was to get the vital signs of the patient after they had been sent to the back to see the doctor. In other words, we would get their chief complaint, take their pulse, blood pressure, and temperature and then write it all down on the pad. Pretty simple stuff.

The doctor would then come in to see the patient. He would then write orders for the patient. The nurse would follow the doctor and carry out whatever the doctor ordered, which could be to give them a shot or some kind of medicine or whatever.

There were several big examining rooms in the emergency center and several small rooms. There were four or five rolling examination tables in the big rooms. Curtains separated the tables to give the patients some measure of privacy.

This particular night, Russell and I were working at tables side-by-side with a curtain between us. The curtain was not pulled all the way back. In other words, the patients could not see each other, but Russell and I could see each other.

My patient was a nine-month old baby who was running a high fever. The baby was screaming at the top of her lungs. Russell's patient was a thirty-five-year-old man who had injured his wrist while playing tennis.

Russell and I were sharing a small adjustable table to put our supplies on while we worked. The table was at the curtain between the two patients.

I was using a rectal thermometer to take the temperature of the little baby. I had no idea what I was doing, but I was somehow getting the job done. I had always left all the rectal temperature taking to my wife at home. In other words, I was being stretched out of my comfort zone. I nervously removed the thermometer, checked the reading, and placed the thermometer on a tissue on the little table we were sharing.

I turned my head for a split second to write down the reading and then looked back and noticed the thermometer was gone. I looked up just in time to see Russell placing the rectal thermometer, Vaseline and all, in his patient's mouth.

The gentleman puckered up like someone had put a dill pickle in his mouth!

"Russell," I tried to say calmly, "I need to talk to you."

"We can talk in a minute," he replied very professionally. "Give me just a minute and let me finish getting the vitals on my patient."

I looked on the little table and noticed another thermometer. I picked it up and noticed in was nice and clean. Trying to keep from laughing, I said, "Russell, you have used the wrong thermometer. You just put my used rectal thermometer in his mouth."

Russell was beginning to smile, but I knew he didn't believe me. "Russell," I said, "Check to see if your patient has a 104 degree temperature."

Russell pulled the thermometer out of the patient's mouth and finally realized what had happened. Russell was baldheaded and had not a hair on his head. I can still see his baldhead turning red as he laughed uncontrollably in the hall.

As Russell was laughing, I went back in the room

and spoke to his patient.

"Sir," I said, "if you tasted a little twang with your thermometer, it is because of the new kind of alcohol we are using."

Until the day he died, I believe Russell thought I somehow purposely played a trick on him to cause all that to happen.

D o c !

Later that same week in that emergency room, a nurse came up to me with a syringe and said, "Bruce, please go in room four and give this shot to the patient."

I had never given anyone a shot in my life, but there was no way I was going to let the nurse think I was incompetent or something. I figured giving a shot couldn't be too difficult.

I actually was wearing a white lab coat with a stethoscope hanging around my neck. I looked fairly professional, I guess, so I thought I could get away with it.

I walked in the little examination room and explained to the man that I was about to give him a shot. He looked to be about my age and did not seem concerned at all. I helped him roll his sleeve up and inserted the needle in his arm.

I cringed when I felt the needle hit a bone. I could see the pain on this poor man's face. I thought at first I had hung the needle in his bone, but I was able to get it out without too much trouble. After I pulled the needle out, I'll never forget this patient's response. "Doggone it, Doc!" he cried, rubbing his aching arm.

If that poor guy had known that I was really an undertaker, he would have passed out.

I think I forgot you are supposed to "pinch" some muscle tissue before inserting the needle.

I watched the man as he paid his bill. I stood at the door and watched him walking to his car in the parking lot. He was rubbing his arm and moving it up and down all the way to his car.

I never heard anymore from him. I hope he didn't lose his arm.

Dealer Downs and Birthing Babies

If one would make a top ten list of the real characters in the history of Reynolds, my good friend Downs Scott would have to be on the list.

Downs is one of those guys that everybody knows and everybody loves. For many years he was in the car-selling business in other towns. But in the middle 70's, he bought the Chevron station in Reynolds and became a Reynolds fixture. However, it was when he later sold that business and started his new business that he became a legend. The name of his business was the Dealer Burger, after the nickname he had acquired in the car business. The menu included the best fried chicken you would ever put in your mouth. But as good as the chicken was, that was not the reason people flocked to his diner.

The crowds came for two reasons: The first reason was because of the conversation you would find there. There was always somebody there with whom you could shoot the bull. The second and biggest reason was because of Downs himself. Downs and his Dealer Burger quickly became an institution in Reynolds. When Downs decided to close the Dealer Burger, a very important chapter in the history of Reynolds closed with it.

If you wanted to know anything and everything about the people of Taylor County, the Dealer Burger was the place to be. It became *the* meeting place in

Reynolds. Nobody cared that they smelled like fried food when they left.

I became acquainted with Downs about the time he was buying the Chevron station. Downs had agreed to assist us in the ambulance service, and he had become an EMT. There was a period of time when Downs and I made about 80% of all the ambulance calls. We would get a call, I would leave the grocery store and Downs would leave his station, and we would meet at the ambulance and take off to wherever we had to go.

I spent many an hour with Downs riding up and down the road in the ambulance. I don't know if we ever saved anybody's life, but we sure solved a lot of the world's problems.

Downs and I had one understanding, and the understanding was this. Whenever we had the threat of a baby being born, I would drive. I didn't want to be caught in the back of the ambulance with a woman having a baby. But sometimes it happened anyway.

One night we got a call that a woman was having a baby and they needed an ambulance 10-18. (10-18 is radio code for "Hurry Up.") I drove the ambulance to the house and was already making plans to be sure I drove to the hospital when we later transported the pregnant lady to the hospital.

We didn't realize it at the time, but my brother Mac, who was our senior EMT, was coming into town when he saw the ambulance leaving. He had followed us to the house. By the time Downs and I got the equipment out and got into the house, Mac was already in the house with the patient.

We discovered that she was over eight months pregnant and had never been to the doctor concerning her pregnancy. The labor pains were getting stronger and closer together. I knew we didn't have much time.

In spite of my objections, Mac decided to drive that night. Downs and I were in the back of the ambulance with a screaming pregnant girl and her screaming mother.

The girl in labor would yell at the top of her lungs. Her mother would yell "Oh, Jesus" right behind her. The pains were getting very close. I asked Downs to stick his head through the sliding window and tell Mac to hurry up.

I pulled the sheet back about that time and the water broke like an explosion – right in my face. I didn't know at the time what had exploded, but whatever it was, it was all over me.

I guess I hollered when it all hit me. Downs had his head stuck through the sliding window talking to Mac and heard me holler. He jerked his head back and knocked himself in the head and ended up with a big knot.

When I got my composure (or some of it), I saw only a foot hanging out of the birth canal. We were almost 25 minutes from the hospital. Downs and I both knew we were in a heap of trouble.

The girl in labor was screaming louder, and her mother was screaming for her to push. I was pleading with her to hold her legs together.

Right in the middle of all that was going on, Downs screamed loudly to be heard over the other screamers and got everybody's attention.

I'll never forget what he said and in such a calm voice, "Do you folks care if I comb my hair?"

And he started combing his hair.

We made it to the hospital with the foot still hanging out. We found out later the baby had been dead for several weeks in the womb.

I don't have any explanation for Down's sudden urge to comb his hair, but his action definitely helped all of us to calm down in the back of the ambulance.

When You Got To Go, You Got To Go!

I suppose this is a good place to go public with a little problem I have – when I have to go, I have to go. My problem has caused many embarrassing moments for my family and me. It has caused me to go into places I would never dream of going. It has caused me to drive faster than I should ever drive. I've run through more convenience stores that O.J. ran through airports. I've been in bathrooms without lights, without paper, without locks, without doors, and, absolutely, without mercy.

My problem runs in my family. I got it honestly. My mother suffered from it, my brothers and sister suffers from it.

On a trip to Atlanta one day, my brother Mac stopped at a stranger's house to use the bathroom. He just knocked on the screen door and asked a man sitting in his easy chair if he could use his bathroom. The man never got up from his chair. He invited him in and pointed down the hall. While he was in the stranger's bathroom, Mac found some Pepto Bismol in his medicine cabinet and took a swig of it. He tried to pay the man for the Pepto Bismol as he was leaving, but he would not accept it.

I'm sure you have heard the saying, "When you got to go, you got to go."

Well, I must tell you. When someone by the name of Goddard has to go, they really have to go. There is no warning and no time think about it.

My wife, Kathy, and my mother-in-law, Irene, drove over with me to Fort Valley one night to eat at the Dairy Queen. There is something about red meat that contributes greatly to my IBS. And the problem is I just love red meat.

I had a double cheeseburger that night – just ketchup – and large fries. We took our time at the Dairy Queen, chatting and enjoying our meal. We left to enjoy a leisurely, fifteen-minute drive back to Reynolds. But, before we could get out of Fort Valley, it hit me.

I pulled over into Smisson's Service Station. I could tell the attendant was turning the lights off and was in the process of closing his business for the night. I ran up to him and frantically asked him if I could use his restroom.

I could tell he was not very happy about it, but he agreed to let me use it. I'm sure he had a long day and was ready to go home.

I was in the bathroom longer than I intended to be. Every time I would try to get up, it would hit me again.

Don't laugh because you know you've been there.

I could tell the gas station attendant was very irritated when I finally came out of the bathroom. My wife and mother-in-law were just as irritated. I apologized to the attendant and to my wife and mother-in-law for keeping them so long, but explained to them I could not help it.

Before I could get the car cranked up, it hit me again.

"Kathy, I hate to tell you this. But I've got to go back to the bathroom!"

Kathy said, "There is no way you are going back in that bathroom!" I agreed and pulled in next door at Bobby's Minit Mart.

I literally ran in this convenience store. The dad of one of my old high-school friends was in the checkout line and tried to talk to me. There was no way I could carry on a conversation with Mr. DeGraw at that point.

I said to the clerk as calmly and as meekly as I could (with chill bumps popping all over my body), "Could you please tell me where your restroom is?"

Her response almost caused me to relax, and that would not have been good. "I'm sorry, but our restroom is for employees only."

My response was quick and to the point. "Then give me an application!"

I think she got the picture. She had two choices. One of them included letting me use the restroom. I'll let you figure out the other choice, but it would have involved her having to close the store. Thankfully, she was a smart lady. She pointed in the direction of the restroom.

It's My Grandmother

My grandmother moved to Reynolds from Ft. Myers, Florida, about the time I graduated from high school. Her name was Mabel Gonzalez, better known to all her grandchildren as "Mama Mabel."

Mama Mabel bought a mobile home and put it in my parents' backyard, so she could be close to my Mama, who was her oldest daughter, in the last years of her life.

Mama Mabel was a no-nonsense type person who always spoke her mind. You never had to wonder about what Mama Mabel thought because she did not mind telling you. For instance, I remember when my brother George brought a girlfriend home one weekend from college. George introduced her to Mama Mabel. As soon as she walked out of the room, George asked Mama Mabel how she liked her.

"I have never heard of a young lady coming to meet the parents of her boyfriend wearing blue jeans!" she said.

George asked her, "What do you think she should have worn?" Mama Mabel replied without any hesitation, "A dress."

That was Mama Mabel.

Mama Mabel had another trait that all of her grandchildren have laughed about many times. She insisted that she never saw herself naked.

We asked her how she took a bath. She would

always say, "I don't look."

I don't know another person in the world who would say they have never seen themselves naked.

But as stern as Mama Mabel was, we had a lot of fun with her, and we (her grandchildren) had a knack for getting her to laugh. I think she would have enjoyed the story I am about to relate.

Mama Mabel was born on Christmas day, she was married on Christmas day, and she died on July 4th. I don't know what all that means, but those are the facts. Her funeral was to be held in Reynolds in the chapel at the funeral home. We planned on having a separate committal service in Fort Myers. When I was setting all this up, I decided it would be useless for me to hire a funeral home in Florida to handle the committal service, so I decided to handle getting everything set up myself from Georgia.

I told my wife, Kathy, that we could carry Mama Mabel to Fort Myers in our personal Astro van. Then we could take our time coming back and make a mini vacation out of it. If we carried the hearse, our options would be very limited.

So after the chapel service, we took all the seats out of Kathy's van and loaded the casket and the flowers in the back. We had to move the seats as forward as they would go to get the casket in the van. The fact that I'm almost 6'5" would make this a very cramped and uncomfortable trip for me. Our plan was to stop at a motel on the way to Fort Myers to breakup the trip. The committal service was to be held the next day.

Kathy and I (and Mama Mabel) left for Ft. Myers a

couple of hours ahead of the rest of the family after the service at the chapel. Our first stop was somewhere near Valdosta, Georgia to get gas. The attendant came out to where I was pumping the gas and looked in the van. I noticed the quizzical look on his face when he asked, "Is that a casket in your van?" I nodded affirmatively.

"It's my grandmother," I said nonchalantly.

I'll never forget his next statement. "You don't use funeral homes where you come from?"

I told him it was much cheaper this way.

Kathy and I were laughing uncontrollably when we got back on the road. We knew this was going to be an eventful trip.

We traveled a lot further than we had planned that night. It was getting pretty late, and we were about ready to find a motel to check in. We stopped at a fast-food restaurant and discovered Ft. Myers was only a couple of hours away. We decided to drive on to Ft. Myers.

When we arrived in Fort Myers, we saw a Ramada Inn that looked decent. I checked in the motel and as we drove around to get to the room, Kathy immediately said there was no way she was going to stay in this run-down motel. It was much worse looking in the back than it looked in the front.

I told Kathy I would try to get my money back, but before I did anything I had to use the bathroom. So Kathy stayed in the van, and I went in the room.

I was in there longer than I anticipated. Kathy finally came in to be sure I was all right. I finally finished, and we went back out to get in the van to find another motel. We quickly discovered the keys were locked in the van. Now we had a major problem.

I knew there was no way to get in that van with a coat hanger. So I went back in the room where Kathy did not want to stay and looked in the yellow pages to find a locksmith. I did find one and gave him a call. It was midnight, but he said he would be right over.

The "right over" turned out to be about an hour later. Kathy had decided to stay in the run-down motel by now. We both were exhausted, but we needed to get our stuff out of the van. We also wanted to be sure we could get Mama Mabel out in time for her burial.

The locksmith finally arrived. He picked the lock in a matter of seconds and opened the back door. He shined his flashlight inside the van.

I didn't give him a chance to say anything. "That's my first wife," I said very calmly.

At the moment those words came out of my mouth, Kathy opened the door of the motel room and asked, "Did you get the door opened?"

The locksmith looked at Kathy and then looked at the casket in the van and said, "I'm not asking any questions."

We laughed ourselves to sleep that night.

The next morning I had to go to the courthouse to pay the cemetery fees for the funeral that day. Since I had no other vehicle, I had to drive the van and take Mama Mabel with me. I left Mama Mabel in the parking lot at the courthouse when I went in to sign papers and give them a check. When I came out of the courthouse and was getting back in the van, I noticed, across the street, Hanson Appraisal Company, a business owned by my cousin. I decided to drive across the street to see if Woody was in. I had no choice but to let Mama Mabel wait in the van again. I intended to visit Woody only a few minutes, but the visit lasted much longer. I forgot about Mama Mabel waiting in the van.

As I was leaving, Woody walked me out to the parking lot. He was telling me that he would be at the service that afternoon. As we walked up to the van, Woody had a funny expression on his face. He asked, "Is that Aunt Mabel?"

I told him I would have brought her in to see him, but I didn't have her pallbearers with me.

In the meantime, Kathy was waiting at the motel and was worried to death that something had happened to me. When I got to the motel, I told her that Mama Mabel and I had been visiting this morning.

It was getting close to the funeral hour, but Kathy and I were about to starve. We decided to go to the Waffle House on the way to the cemetery. Mama Mabel again waited in the van in the Waffle House parking lot while we ate omelets.

After we finished eating, we decided, since Mama Mabel had been all over Ft. Myers, that the least we should do would be to ride her by her old house on the way to the cemetery. So, Kathy and I took Mama Mabel on a little tour of Ft. Myers on the way to the cemetery.

When we finally arrived at the cemetery, Kathy and I were still laughing about this incredible trip and the fact that it could be made into a movie. We knew Mama Mabel was laughing with us from heaven, but we also knew she was ready for us to get her to her final resting place so she could finally rest in peace.

As I was turning the van around so I could back up to the lowering device at the grave, I backed into a concrete pole. I got out and realized that the back door of the van was jammed.

After some creative body work on that vehicle, I finally got the door opened, and we did get Mama Mabel buried that day. But I will never forget that trip as long as I live.

Chapter Four

YOU WILL HAVE TROUBLE

"I don't care how old you are, what you do for a living, the color of your skin, or whether you live in Chicago or Reynolds. Things won't always go your way. You can just mark that down as truth. If you don't believe it, just wait."

God, Where Are You?

The world ain't gonna stop when you die, and we need to lighten up. It really is ok to laugh. In fact – it's good for you. But let me tell you something else I've learned about life, viewing it from my hearse.

In this world, you are going to have trouble.

I don't care how old you are, what you do for a living, the color of your skin, or whether you live in Chicago or Reynolds, Georgia. Things won't always go your way. You can just mark that down as truth. If you don't believe it, just wait.

I've noticed that, viewing life from my hearse. But I've also read it in the Bible. Jesus himself said it. "In this world you will have trouble."(John 16:13). He didn't say you might. He said you would.

I have noticed some things about people going through trouble. I've dealt with people going through trouble all my life. I've dealt with this thing we call death since I was a little kid.

I've never lost a mate or a child, but I've walked through that experience with many people. I cannot imagine the pain people feel in those situations. I do know it has to be very, very hard.

But the older I get, the more I realize that people go through trouble that has nothing to do with death. Sometimes the pain we experience in the circumstances of life can probably be just as bad as the physical loss of a loved one.

One of the things I have noticed is that most of us, when trouble comes, have the tendency to push away from it. "What in the world did I do to deserve this? Why is this happening to me? Why am I in this financial mess? Why are my kids in this mess? Why am I feeling like this?"

"God, where are you?"

Have you ever asked that question?

If you have, then you need to be sure to read the rest of this book.

Think with me for a moment. Can you imagine what this world would be like if all we had were sunshine and it never rained?

I'm not a farmer and probably not very smart, but I don't think anything would grow.

Or if all we had was daytime and it never got night?

I'm convinced, viewing life from my hearse, that it takes the rain and the sunshine, it takes the night and the day, it takes the hard times and the good times, to make us whoever God meant for us to be.

I also want you to know that the worst thing you can do when trouble comes, is to push away from it.

I want you to think about the worst thing you have ever gone through in your life.

I understand that everybody has a different story. For some it has been worse than others. I understand that. Some of you might have never gotten over what you went through. I understand that. The truth is you might never get over it. For some of you, you are right in the middle of the worst thing you've ever gone through. I understand that, too.

But, if you think about the worst thing you have

ever gone through, and you are honest, it was a step-pingstone – (or it will be a steppingstone) to take you places you could never have gone, to allow you to help people you could never have helped unless you went through whatever it is you had to go through.

I am absolutely convinced of that truth. All things really do work together for the good for those who love God and have been called according to His purpose.

I am keenly aware that for some of you reading this book, it is pouring down rain in your life. I know that's true. It could be all kinds of things.

I'm thinking about broken relationships with your mate, children, grandchildren, or old friends. It could be financial pressures. It could be physical illness. It could be loneliness and depression. I could get up a big list, but I think you know what I am talking about.

Some of you, if you really told the truth, don't even want tomorrow to get here because of what you are facing. I just know that is true.

But for some of you, the sun is shining. I'm happy for you. I am really glad things seem to be going your way. But I will just go ahead and tell you.

It's going to rain again. You can absolutely count on it.

Sometimes I turn on my TV early on Sunday mornings, and I hear theology that makes me very nervous. I hear things like if you have your life in order, you will not experience trouble. When you hear that, throw a brick through your TV if that is what it takes to turn it off. It is hogwash.

I understand that we bring trouble on ourselves.

When we do stupid things, we will reap the conse-
quences. We reap what we sow.

The laws of God are very similar to the laws of
nature. If you throw a ball against a wall, I can tell you
before you throw it that the ball is going to come back
to you.

But I also know that some balls come your way
when you have not thrown one yourself.

Do you remember the story when Jesus sent his
disciples out in the boat?

They did exactly what He told them to do. They got
out in the middle of the lake, and they experienced the
storm of their lives. Whatever they were worried about
before they got in that boat, they forgot quickly.

Their chief objective was to survive through the
storm. All their energy was directed at keeping the
boat from turning over.

And they were asking, "Where is Jesus? Why did
he allow this to happen? Why is this happening to us?
Did we do something wrong? Didn't he tell us to take
the boat out?"

Have you ever been there?

I have.

In the middle of the worst of my storms, God used
an author named Max Lucado to show me the little
story about the disciples and the boat.

My life would be forever changed.

I realized in a very new and real way, if God didn't
come through, I was sunk.

It was that simple. I was fighting to survive. All my
energy was being spent in my attempt to keep from
drowning. And I was asking from the depths of my

heart, "God, where are you?"

And in a supernatural moment, He showed me.

Jesus was standing on the seashore. He was watching the disciples. He had not gone anywhere. And at just the right time, He would show up and calm the storm. In fact, the Bible says that he went up on the mountainside to pray. He was not only watching His disciples in the storm, He was praying for them as well!

I realized that God was watching me, and He was concerned about me. And He had a purpose for my life that I could not even begin to comprehend, just as He had a purpose for those disciples. God had brought me to this place of desperation.

I knew that God was getting ready to use me. I did not understand the details, but I knew it was true. I believed in a way I had never understood before that everything I had ever experienced was for a reason, and God would use all of it to fulfill my purpose for being on the earth.

I knew I had always loved to laugh. For some reason I have always had the ability to see the lighter side. But I also knew that God had given me a heart for Him. I almost felt like the two were in conflict with each other. I also knew I was created to be in funeral service. I was trained and mentored all my life to serve people in the most difficult time of their lives through the funeral business. And I loved it. But owning a funeral business, with all the financial obligations and bondage that came with it, was the thing that was keeping me from being set free to be who God created me to be.

I was beginning to think, "Is it possible for God to

take my experience in running a funeral business, my craziness, and my heart for Him and use them all together to make a difference in my world?" Over the next several years, the answer began to come.

It all started slowly. I was asked to speak to the Taylor County Ministerial Association Christmas banquet in Butler, Georgia. I told some of my funny experiences you have read in this book, and I shared a little of my heart from my unique perspective on life. They laughed so hard! But I also saw tears. Somebody heard about my little talk with the ministers, and I was asked to go to a civic club and then another club and then to a banquet and the invitations kept coming. And I sensed very strongly that God was going before me.

After a few years of an ever-increasing number of speaking invitations, I acted on what I believed with all my heart God showed me at the height of my storm and desperation. I sold our 130-year-old funeral business. I was hired by the company who bought it to continue to run the funeral homes, which was neat for me, but now I was not tied down financially and had time and opportunity to cultivate my God-given gifts in more and more opportunities to speak. After eight months, the new company sold to a large public company, and I found myself all of a sudden working in corporate America in the funeral business with an opportunity to take my gifts and my message all across the country to an audience I had never dreamed.

You see, God used the greatest storm of my life to be the greatest thing that ever happened to me. I was forced to look at some things in a way I never would unless the pressure was there to make me look. I made decisions I never would have made unless I was forced to make those decisions.

I want to be sure you understand. Before the storm, I owned and operated two funeral homes that represented about 70 funerals per year (in a good year), and I had never spoken publicly in my life.

Today, as I write this, I have personal operational responsibility for over 140 funeral homes and cemeteries in eight states, from Georgia to Oklahoma. Those funeral homes represent 18,000 funerals annually, and the cemeteries represent 12,000 interments per year. And to date, I have had over 900 speaking engagements all the way from Oregon to Georgia.

All this transpired as a result of the storm in my life that forced me to stop in my tracks and to seek help from the man who standing on the seashore watching me struggle.

I said all this to make a very important point. You really need to hear this.

God has a purpose for your life. He uses every experience life has to offer to make you the person God created you to be. You will most definitely have trouble in this life. But the trouble comes for a reason – and for a season.

Every time I stand in front of a crowd and almost every time I board an airplane to go to visit a funeral home or a cemetery, I think of that terrible storm that consumed my life. And I am reminded over and over that just as He did for the disciples, at just the right time, He came and calmed my storm, and set me free to be who He created me to be.

The worst thing that ever happened to me became the best thing that ever happened.

That is God's way.

If you are hurting and dismayed and you are desperately rowing your boat in the midst of your storm, I want you remind you that God hasn't gone anywhere. He is watching. And He cares for you. And he is more than able to calm your storm. In fact, He is your only hope.

And He will take the worst thing that ever happened to you, and use it for His glory and for your good. That is the way He works. That is the way He worked yesterday. And that is the way He will work tomorrow.

That you can count on.

What Does the Bible Say?

Although God showed me the big picture in the storm I have just shared with you, the storms keep coming. Sometimes I bring the storms on myself and sometimes they just come, but the storms keep coming.

Sometimes it rains, sometimes the sun is shining, and sometimes it is overcast. Sometimes the sun shines brightly, and we bask in it. Sometimes the rain is gentle, and we play in it. Sometimes the sun is so hot we cannot bear it. And sometimes the rain and wind are so hard, we have to take shelter to be protected from them.

We can learn a lot about God and the life He has given us by looking at the world He has established.

But don't ever let anyone ever tell you that the sun is supposed to shine all the time. It is a ludicrous thought, and it is ludicrous to God.

He never promised we would have no storms. But He did promise that He would be with us in the midst of them.

God is our refuge and strength, an ever-present help in trouble. Therefore we will not fear, though the earth give way and the mountains fall into the heart of the sea, though its waters roar and foam and the mountains quake with their surging.

There is a river whose streams make glad the city of God, the holy place where the Most High dwells. God is within her, she will not fall; God will help her at break of day. Nations are in uproar, kingdoms fall; he lifts his voice, the earth melts. The LORD Almighty is with us; the God of Jacob is our fortress. (**Psalms 46: 2-7 NIV**)

Do you not know? Have you not heard? The LORD is the everlasting God, the Creator of the ends of the earth. He will not grow tired or weary, and his understanding no one can fathom. He gives strength to the weary and increases the power of the weak. Even youths grow tired and weary, and young men stumble and fall; but those who hope in the LORD will renew their strength. They will soar on wings like eagles; they will run and not grow weary, they will walk and not be faint. **(Isaiah 40:28-31 NIV)**

Therefore, since we have been justified through faith, we have peace with God through our Lord Jesus Christ, through whom we have gained access by faith into this grace in which we now stand. And we rejoice in the hope of the glory of God. Not only so, but we also rejoice in our sufferings, because we know that suffering produces perseverance; perseverance, character; and character, hope. And hope does not disappoint us, because God has poured out his love into our hearts by the Holy Spirit, whom he has given us. **(Romans 5:1-5 NIV)**

Praise be to the God and Father of our Lord Jesus Christ! In his great mercy he has given us new birth into a living hope through the resurrection of Jesus Christ from the dead, and into an inheritance that can never perish, spoil or fade – kept in heaven for you, who through faith are shielded by God's power until the coming of the salvation that is ready to be revealed in the last time. In this you greatly rejoice, though now for a little while you may have had to suffer grief in all kinds of trials. These have come so that your faith – of greater worth than gold, which perishes even though refined by fire – may be proved genuine and may result in praise, glory and honor when Jesus Christ is revealed. Though you have not seen him, you love him; and even though you do not see him now, you believe in him and are filled with an inexpressible and glorious joy, for you are receiving the goal of your faith, the salvation of your souls. **(I Peter 1:3-9 NIV)**

We are hard pressed on every side, but not crushed; perplexed, but not in despair; persecuted, but not abandoned; struck down, but not destroyed. **(2 Corinthians 4:8-9 NIV)**

Therefore we do not lose heart. Though outwardly we are wasting away, yet inwardly we are being renewed day by day. For our light and momentary troubles are achieving for us an eternal glory that far outweighs them all. So we fix our eyes not on what is seen, but on what is unseen. For what is seen is temporary, but what is unseen is eternal. **(2 Corinthians 4: 16-18 NIV)**

Who shall separate us from the love of Christ? Shall trouble or hardship or persecution or famine or nakedness or danger or sword? As it is written: "For your sake we face death all day long; we are considered as sheep to be slaughtered." No, in all these things we are more than conquerors through him who loved us. For I am convinced that neither death nor life, neither angels nor demons, neither the present nor the future, nor any powers, neither height nor depth, nor anything else in all creation, will be able to separate us from the love of God that is in Christ Jesus our Lord. **(Romans 8:35-39 NIV)**

I learned a very powerful poem that speaks to this thing we call trouble. It is one of the most powerful things I ever learned. I have quoted it many times over the years for thousands of people. I take great delight and comfort as I watch people get completely blown away by the truth in the words penned by Rudyard Kipling:

If

If you can keep your head when all about you
Are losing theirs and blaming it on you,
If you can trust yourself when all men
  doubt you
But make allowance for their doubting too,
If you can wait and not be tired by waiting,
Or being lied about, don't deal in lies,
Or being hated, don't give way to hating,
And yet don't look too good,
  nor talk too wise:
If you can dream – and not make dreams
  your master,
If you can think – and not make thoughts
your aim;
If you can meet with Triumph and Disaster
And treat those two impostors just the same;
If you can bear to hear the truth
  you've spoken
Twisted by knaves to make a trap for fools,
Or watch the things you gave
  your life to, broken,
And stoop and build 'em up with
  worn-out tools:
If you can make one heap of all
  your winnings
And risk it all on one turn of pitch-and-toss,
And lose, and start again at your beginnings
And never breath a word about your loss;
If you can force your heart and nerve

and sinew
To serve your turn long after they are gone,
And so hold on when there is nothing in you
Except the Will which says to them:
    "Hold on!"
If you can talk with crowds and keep
    your virtue,
Or walk with kings – nor lose the
    common touch,
If neither foes nor loving friends can hurt you;
If all men count with you, but none too much,
If you can fill the unforgiving minute
With sixty seconds' worth of distance run,
Yours is the Earth and everything that's in it,
And – which is more – you'll be a Man,
    my son!
– *Rudyard Kipling*

Chapter Five

INVESTMENTS THAT WILL LAST

"I don't remember a word they said . . . But I sure do remember what they did."

The Braves Won Last Night!

The world ain't gonna stop when you die. We need to lighten up. In this world you will have trouble. All those statements are so true. But there is another observation I've made about life, viewing it from my hearse. If you don't hear anything else I've said, you really need to hear this.

The only investments you will make in this life that will be here when you are dead and gone and some crazy guy like me buries you, are the investments you make in people.

Listen to this country undertaker, because I'm telling you the truth.

There is nothing wrong with making money. You better make money. I understand about money. I have two kids in college and one that just got finished – and a wife that likes to shop. Believe me, I understand about money.

I know it is important to invest your money wisely. That is a biblical concept, and I know it is important. But financial investment principles are for another book by another author.

But I will tell you this. If your chief focus in life is to see how much money you can make and to see how many things you can accumulate, you will get to the end of your life and you will realize that you missed the boat.

I've walked away from a lot of cemeteries. As I

write this, I feel like I deal with death almost every minute of every day.

I don't think I have ever seen a family walk away from the scene at a graveside service and look back and say, "I wish Daddy would have spent more time at the office."

You don't ever hear that.

What you do hear is, "I wish I had five more minutes with Daddy" or "I wish I had five more minutes with Mama."

I can tell you honestly. I wish *I* had five more minutes with Daddy and five more minutes with Mama.

I used to play basketball. I worked hard at playing basketball and actually got pretty good at it. What used to amaze me is that whenever my team had traveled to a game and was walking in a gym, no matter where we were playing, my Mama would walk in right behind us. I don't ever remember her missing a basketball game. I'm sure she did, but I don't remember it.

There was another thing I noticed during my basketball-playing years that was actually more amazing than my Mama coming to basketball games. Most of the time it would happen before the game started. Sometimes it may have been after the game had begun, but I would look up and see my Daddy walk in that gym. Many of those times he would be wearing a dark suit. I knew he was a busy man. And I knew he had traveled a long way to a basketball game. My thinking back then was, "Daddy must love basketball!"

But I got a little older and got married and started having kids of my own, and I realized it was not basketball Daddy was so interested in. What he was interested in were those people that God had entrusted to him. And he spent his life, invested his life, in those people.

My Mama was a very special lady. I don't mind telling you that I absolutely loved my Mama. When she was dying at the Medical Center in Macon, Georgia, we were gathered around her bed. My two brothers, Mac and George, and my sister, Kikky, were there, as were our wives and Kikky's husband. Mama was gasping for breath. For a couple of days, we all thought every breath would be her last. The truth is, at that point, we were praying that every breath would be her last so she could just go "home."

But early one morning, she sort of woke up. She called my name. I am the youngest of the four children, but I'm a big boy. I started to get people out of the way. I had a strong feeling that this would be the last thing she ever said to me, and I wanted to be sure I heard it. I bent over and put my ear to her dry, parched lips. I barely could understand what she was saying. But I heard her. You are not going to believe what she told me. It was the last thing she ever said to me.

In a very weak voice, she whispered, "The Braves won last night."

"The Braves won last night! Mama! Who cares right now that the Braves won last night for goodness sakes!" (I'll have to admit I did ask her what the score was).

I later started thinking about the last thing she ever told me.

The truth is my Mama was the biggest Braves fan

you would ever meet in your life. In 1969, when the Atlanta Braves won the National League Western Division for the first time, my Mama got in her car at midnight and drove up and down the streets of Reynolds honking the horn. You talk about a Braves fan.

My brother George and I went to the University of Georgia. When we started to school there, Mama didn't know a football from a tennis ball. I remember coming home one Saturday when Georgia was playing on the road. We caught her standing in the den in front of the television by herself, screaming at the top of her lungs, "Throw the ball, Dooley!" We didn't say anything, but we were thinking, "Mama, football?"

The truth is the last thing she told me is very important to me today. Her whole life was wrapped up in those people that God had entrusted to her. She had become the biggest Braves fan you would ever meet and the biggest Georgia Bulldog fan, because that's what her kids were doing.

I didn't say it then, but I thought it later: "Mama, I don't know if the Braves won. But *you* won."

And she did.

Pictures

I read a book many years ago that included a quote that greatly impacted my life. I wish I could give credit to the person who made this statement, but I don't remember the name of the book or the person who gave it to me. But I remember the quote:

"Pictures have a way of changing you. Far more profoundly and far more permanently than words ever could."

I have never forgotten the truth that resounds in that quote.

I remember my grade-school teachers. I can name them all. Mrs. Mattie Emma Ogburn, Mrs. Verna Fountain, Mrs. Wilma Hollis, Mrs. Mabel Byrd, Mrs. Susie Woods, Mrs. Lucibelle Fuller, Mrs. Mildred Payne, Mrs. Betty Whatley and Mrs. Ruth Jones.

I can tell you that special group of ladies greatly impacted my life and the lives of many others who went through that school in Reynolds.

They taught us reading and writing and arithmetic. As I mentioned at the beginning of this book, the older I get the more I realize just how well they did that. But they taught us much, much more. To them, teaching was not just a job for a paycheck; they literally invested their lives in those kids who were entrusted to them.

I have so many mental pictures of these special ladies. I wish there was a way I could put those pictures in this book, but it would be impossible because they are not on photo paper. But they are indelibly printed in my mind – and in my heart.

But I have to tell you a crazy thing.

I don't remember a word they said. I've sat down and tried to remember some of their words, but I am hard-pressed to think of anything. And I'm not stupid.

But I sure do remember what they did. And I remember the way they made me feel.

I remember my Sunday school teachers at the Reynolds United Methodist Church. I've buried all of them but one. Whenever they had Sunday school, I was there. The teachers hauled us to pizza parlors, ice cream parlors, and bowling alleys time and time again. And they taught us Sunday after Sunday. But you know what?

I don't remember a lesson they taught.

I know I picked up principles along the way. But the truth is I don't remember what they said. But I sure do remember what they did – and I remember the way they made me feel.

Folks, we have the words down pat. We are good with the speeches. We know what to say to our kids or grandkids to pat them on the rear end to send them on the way. We even know what to say to our neighbor who is in trouble. We do great with the speeches. We can talk the talk.

I hate to tell you this, but those people that God has entrusted to you won't remember much of what you said. I worked with my Daddy every day of my adult life until he died. I remember some of what he said. But I have a whole lot more pictures of what he did.

Remember, I'm not a preacher – I'm an undertaker. But there is not a more biblical thing for some of you dads and granddads to do than to go outside with that little boy and throw that ball. Or go to that little league game or that soccer game, or fishing hole, or whatever it is you do.

And there is not a more important thing for you moms and grandmothers, than to take that little girl in the kitchen and teach her how to make bread, or a pound cake, or to balance a checkbook, or take the trip to the mall.

The pictures you create for those people will live on long after you are dead and gone. All the speeches – I hate to tell you, but they won't remember them.

My dad and mom are dead and gone. I understand that, and I've accepted it. I believe they are alive in heaven. But I want to tell you something else. They are alive on this earth, because they are alive in their four children whom they invested their lives in.

And as long as I have breath, I will keep them alive.

We Have This Moment

I have never met anyone yet who does it right all the time. I've met many people who want me to think they do it right all the time. But I know they blow it just like I do. The biggest problem with most churches is many members have this attitude: "We've got our lives together. Come join us and get your life together."

The truth is, nobody has his life together. We are all hopeless and helpless except for the grace of God. None of us measures up. Not one! From Genesis to Revelation, that is the message of the Bible.

I want you to know that there are a lot of things I'm not. I'm not a perfect husband. If you don't believe me, you can ask my imperfect wife. I'm not a perfect daddy. If you don't believe that, you can ask any of my three imperfect children. I'm not a perfect business-man. If you don't believe that, you can ask the people that I work for or those who work for me. The truth is I'm not a perfect anything.

But there is something else I'm not.

I'm not ashamed of the gospel of Jesus Christ. That is the true gospel, the gospel of grace. That gospel is my motivation in causing laughter and tears as I travel all over sharing my views. And that is my motivation in writing this book.

As a result of my understanding of that gospel, I am afraid that we spend too much of our time worrying about how we blew it twenty years ago, or ten years ago, or maybe yesterday. Or maybe we are so worried about what is going to happen tomorrow, or next week, or ten years down the road – that we miss the moment.

I just have to tell you this.

That's all we've got.

But we've got that!

We have this moment.

And everyone has been entrusted with people. Nobody is exempt from that. For some it is your mate, or children, or grandchildren. For some it is your church family, or Sunday school class, or civic club, or neighborhood. Or maybe it is the people you work for or the people that work for you.

But everybody has been entrusted with people.

And all you have is this moment.

Gloria Gaither said it about as well as it can be said in this song:

WE HAVE THIS MOMENT

Lyrics by Gloria Gaither

Hold tight to the sound of the music of living,
Happy songs from the laughter of children
    at play;
Hold my hand as we run through the sweet
    fragrant meadows,
Making mem'ries of what was today.
Tiny voice that I hear is my little girl calling
For Daddy to hear just what she has to say;

My little son running there by the hillside,
May never be quite like today.
Tender words, gentle touch, and a good cup
    of coffee
And someone that loves me and wants
    me to stay;
Hold them near while they're here,
    And don't wish for tomorrow,
To look back and wish for today.
Take the blue of the sky and the green
    of the forest,
And the gold and the brown of the
    freshly mown hay,
Add the pale shades of spring and the
    circus of autumn,
And weave you a lovely today .
We have this moment to hold in our hands,
And to touch as it slips through our fingers
    like sand;
Yesterday's gone, and tomorrow may
    never come,
But we have this moment today.